UNIX® and XENIX®
for beginners

Gerd Küveler

Abacus

A Data Becker Book

Second Printing, May 1990
Printed in U.S.A.

Copyright © 1989, 1990 Abacus
                        5370 52nd Street, S.E.
                        Grand Rapids, MI 49512

Copyright © 1989, 1990 Data Becker GmbH
                        Merowingerstrasse 30
                        4000 Duesseldorf, West Germany

Microsoft, MS-DOS and XENIX are trademarks or registered trademarks of Microsoft Corporation. UNIX is a registered trademark of Bell Laboratories.

ISBN   1-55755-065-4

Table of Contents

Introduction

This introduction to the UNIX Operating System is aimed at people who previously had little or no UNIX experience. Basic knowledge of the following topics is assumed: functional construction of a computer, input/output processing, coding, file access, peripheral equipment (hard disk drive, printer, display terminal) and the difference between software and hardware.

The familiarity with another operating system, especially MS-DOS (or PC-DOS) which is similar to UNIX, makes understanding this material easier, but it is not a prerequisite. The same is true for understanding at least one programming language.

The availability of a UNIX computer would be a great advantage where the concepts learned in this book could be tried out. Most of the training problems require a UNIX computer.

If the solutions cannot be worked out on the computer, the answers, or suggestions about finding a solution, will normally follow the problems. The first three chapters are theoretical in nature and serve for orientation.

Chapter 4 starts a practical approach to UNIX: signing on the system, simple commands and user communications.

Chapters 5 and 6 have a central significance in this introduction. They explain the architecture and practical usage of the file system. Chapter 7 describes the wildcard and Chapter 8 discusses filters and pipes.

Chapter 9 provides a selection of important UNIX commands.

Chapter 10 discusses multi-user operations.

Chapter 11 contains text editors which are available as part of the UNIX operating system.

Chapter 12 provides an introduction into shell programming. Using the operating system is made easier by writing procedures called scripts.

Chapter 13 presents a brief introduction to the C programming language.

Chapter 14 presents features of UNIX and discusses some common UNIX applications.

The appendicies contain additional aides for practical usage of the system.

Throughout this book you will notice icons, small descriptive pictures, in the margin. These icons tell you what to do, whether it is to simply read, note important information or actually enter something at your computers keyboard.

 Reading icon

 Note important information icon

 Exercise icon

 Keyboard entry icon

 Disk icon

 Program listing icon

1. What is an Operating System?

UNIX is a modern day operating system. But, what is an operating system? One definition of an operating system is:

"the programs of a digital computer system which, together with the characteristics of the computer system, form the basis of the various operational modes of the digital computer system and especially those which control and supervise the processing of programs."

This compact and comprehensive description assumes the understanding of some concepts. The "digital computer system" is the hardware. These are the physical components of the computer which can be touched. Thirty years ago this description would have been sufficient. Today additional concepts are required. Besides the "body," a computer system must have a "soul". Since a "soul" must be immaterial, it can only consist of software in a computer. This software is the operating system.

Therefore, the characteristics, better yet the hardware characteristics of the computer system, together with the operating system (software) form the "basis of the processing capabilities." The operating system does not include all the software which can run on a computer. Only the basic software is included in the operating system. This is the software which permits the user of a system to execute the application software specifically written to be used with that operating system. The user of a modern computer system is no longer confronted by the hardware, but with the operating system such as UNIX.

The definition of an operating system above spoke of various operating modes. From the viewpoint of the user, there are three basic operating modes:

• Batch processing

• Conversational (or interactive) mode

• Real-time processing

Batch processing originated during the time when executable programs were read on a card reader in the form of a punched card deck, consisting of control statements and the actual program. The punched cards have now disappeared - at best they can still be found as scraps for notes - but the concept and the operating mode remains.

1

Batch jobs

A batch job must be defined completely and in the proper sequence. The control statements (if required) are usually stored in a file. One of these statements calls the program to be executed. Several programs can be initiated within a batch job. However, all required operating devices such as disk storage, magnetic tape storage, printer, plotter, etc. must be requested from inside the job. No calls to the operating system are permitted since they are not answered.

Batch processing

Batch processing hasn't decreased in significance. An important example is the income tax calculation program used in data processing systems of many accounting departments. The data relevant to the income tax calculations is stored in files. The program obtains all input data it requires from this file. Another important example is the evaluation of the government census data. Here the collected census data was stored in files on magnetic tapes. Since interactive processing was not used, the data did not appear on a screen and unauthorized access was prevented. Thus, the decision in favor of batch processing can be influenced by data security.

Interactive mode

The UNIX operating system also has batch processing capabilities, even though UNIX is an interactive oriented system. No modern operating system is conceivable without dialog between the user and the operating system. This means there is a dialog between the computer (to be more precise the software) and the user. A station is required for every user to input his dialog. In the early days of computers, a Teletypewriter (TTY) was used for the user dialog. Today, terminals with display screens are used. After prompting by a program (not necessarily the operating system), the user enters commands or data with the keyboard of the terminal. This input of data triggers some action in the computer. For example, the display of the departure time of an airline flight from the United States to Paris. In a good interactive operation the answers should appear quickly - within one or two seconds - or the interest of the user may slacken. This is a harsh requirement, since in many cases, several hundred users can be involved in this dialog. Therefore, it is no surprise that the interactive method of operation was developed only long after batch processing.

Real-time processing

Real-time processing also represents a form of dialog which is not between computer and a person, but between computer and devices. An automated system for data acquisition in a laboratory can serve as an example. It is important that certain devices provide results in a fixed time interval, perhaps 1/100 second, and that the computer (often a special process computer) is able to accept them.

During interactive operations, the timing is heavily influenced by the number of active users, especially the length of response times. During real-time operations nothing can influence the pre-set timing. The real-time operation represents a special operating mode which is almost incompatible with the other two. Only some special operating systems are capable of real-time operations. Most modern general operating systems permit the batch and interactive operations - as does UNIX - but they are generally not capable of real-time operations by nature. On some computers it is possible to mix different operating systems for certain applications. For example, an interactive system can be used for program development and a real-time system for program execution.

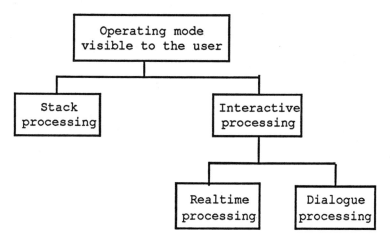

Figure 1

The computer has a different view of the operating modes. An individual may be indifferent to being the only user, or having to share the resources with many other persons, unless it affects the response time or the availability of a resource. The difference is, however, very important to the operating system. Single-user operation and single-

3

processing (only one program at a time) is always easier to implement than multi-user, multi-processing operations.

Well known single-user, single-processing operating systems within the microcomputer world are CP/M (Control Program for 8-bit Microprocessors) and MS-DOS (Microsoft-Disk Operating System for 16-bit processors). MS-DOS or PC-DOS have become the standard of the PC world.

The IBM or IBM-compatible PCs normally run under the familiar DOS operating system. The command and file system structure of DOS is very similar to UNIX, and becomes even more similar to UNIX with each new version. However, DOS is easier to learn and represents good training for the UNIX environment. Those who have mastered DOS already will have less problems studying this book. All large computer systems and most of the middle size installations (Minicomputers or Minis), provide multi-user, multi-processing operating systems. The system handles many users at the same time, each capable of running several programs simultaneously.

In reality, the processor can handle only one program at any one time. The multi-processing characteristic can be implemented with a time-slicing principle. Every program is allocated on the processor for only a few milliseconds and then the next program gets its share of time. The user, working in interactive mode, doesn't notice that his program is inactive most of the time. The computer can typically process the incoming data much faster than a single user can type on a keyboard. Thus, the computer generally spends a large percentage of its time just waiting for input.

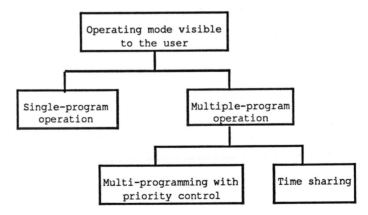

Figure 2

Priority control is a modification of the time-slice principle. Tasks with a higher priority are serviced more frequently. This allows a multi-processing system to use the hardware of the computer more efficiently. Of course, such a system can be difficult to implement. The development time for large scale operating systems such as MVS from IBM, or BS2000 from Siemens, required hundreds of man-years. The storage space requirement is also very high. UNIX, as a multi-user, multi-processing system, was originally intended mainly for use on mini-computers. Such systems typically had a 32-bit microprocessor with 4 to 32 MB of main memory, and supporting 5 to 100 users.

The tasks of an operating system are many. Primarily it must insure the frictionless execution of competing processes or programs with optimal utilization of the available hardware. Deadlocks must be avoided: If Process 1 writes into file A and demands access to file B, while Process 2 writes into file B and requests access to file A -- then nothing will get accomplished in the system.

A "hard core" or Kernel portion of the operating system must be active constantly in main memory. Additional, lessor used portions of the operating system can then reside on disk until required. On demand, these disk resident portions of the operating system software can be loaded into memory and executed when needed. This same "demand paging" technique can also be used to manage memory usage by the application programs running under the operating system. Sharing and partitioning of memory in this way makes more efficient usage of system resources in a dynamic multi-tasking, multi-user environment.

The permanently loaded portions of the operating system software usually include the task scheduler and command processor which maintain communication with the user. The command processor produces the input prompt on your screen, such as "A>" for MS-DOS or "$" for UNIX systems. This prompt may vary from system to system as its generally programmable. In any event, the command entered by the user will activate a specific system function or execute a given application program. Any additional arguments entered on the command line are generally passed on to the executable program by the command processor. A very common command found in some form or another on almost any system is the COPY command to transfer data.

For MS-DOS systems, a typical copy command might be copy A B to copy the contents of file A to file B. UNIX uses a slightly different format of cp   a   b to accomplish the same task. The syntax differs, but the end result is the same. The program used to execute the COPY command is executed by the command processor and the input prompt reappears when the task is done.

The following chapters describe the specific characteristics of the UNIX operating system.

2.   UNIX and MS-DOS, CP/M or OS/2

It can be assumed that a significant number of readers have experience with one of the widely distributed microcomputer operating systems such as CP/M, but mainly MS-DOS or PC-DOS. For this reason, it is useful to point out the similarities and differences as was touched upon at the end of the last section. Knowledge of DOS should help make it a little easier to understand UNIX. At the same time, the capabilities of the various operating systems should become evident.

UNIX is the oldest of the three systems, even though it has been discussed (positively) only in the last few years. CP/M and MS-DOS are oriented strongly towards the main features of UNIX.

The newer versions of MS-DOS resemble UNIX very much. Even the command syntax is very similar. The largest step in the direction of UNIX came with DOS Version 2.0.

Viewed from the user's perspective, the file systems of UNIX and DOS resemble each other a lot. Both originate in a root and are structured hierarchically (like a tree). Directories permit the user to retain an overview. Besides the common files and directories, UNIX also knows an additional type, the device file. Device files provide an interface to the physical devices (for example display, printer, hard disk drive) which are addressed just like an ordinary file (read and write). Special systems call for control of the peripherals and are therefore not required.

Internally a UNIX file differs from a CP/M or DOS file. The orientation toward the record and block structure of a disk has been dropped. UNIX recognizes only blocks which contain byte chains. The type of file (object program, text file, etc.) does not make any difference to UNIX, since it is only a concern of the application program using the file.

The biggest difference from the two "smaller brothers" is in the multi-user capabilities of UNIX. Several users, or even several hundred users, can share the computational capabilities of the system through the terminals. At the same time, every user can execute many tasks in the background (multi-programming). However, on CP/M and MS-DOS systems, single user and single program operation should not be considered a disadvantage. In many cases the PCs are used as truly "personal" computers. Of course the single user operating systems only use a fraction of the output capability of the hardware in the computer.

The processing time of individual components consists mainly of pauses, waiting for data to be processed.

A clear advantage of UNIX against all other systems lies in its portability. This means you can transfer programs and data to other computer types with different processors. This again is based on the fact that UNIX was written in a higher level language (C) and only a small fraction of the system kernel was produced in the processor dependent assembler language. In an extreme contrast, MS-DOS is restricted to the 8086 processor family from INTEL, since it was written in a machine specific assembler language. A switch to the more capable 68000 family from Motorola, while preserving full compatibility, is not possible or at least not a very easy task.

A series of common features exists between UNIX and MS-DOS which should not be ignored. The command processor COMMAND.COM found in MS-DOS is analogous to the shell in UNIX, which is a bit more capable.

Batch processing, meaning the storage of command sequences in a batch file which can be executed, is possible in either system. Even regular programs with structures and loops can be created. Even here UNIX in general offers more capabilities.

The following two tables compare the three standard operating systems for microprocessors: CP/M, MS-DOS and UNIX. UNIX is primarily used in medium and large systems, and is even available on mainframes such as the IBM series 30xx.

Word width	8-bit	8/16-bit	16-bit	16/32-bit	32-bit
Microprocessors	*8080 *Z80	*8080	*8086 *Z8000	*M6800 *32032 *80286 *32016	*M68020 *Z80000 *80386 *32032
Operating system	CP/M	MS-DOS	UNIX		
Systems	Single-user			Multiple-user	

Operating system

Operating systems	CP/M 80	MS-DOS	UNIX 3.3
Complete system	100KB	400 KB	over 8 MB
Resident portion of operating system	8-12 KB	12-35 KB	200-1000 KB
System call	40 KB	100 KB	60 KB
Commands & transient programs	10 KB	50 KB	over 200 KB

Figure 3

For some time now UNIX has been offered in the XENIX version on many PC systems as an alternative to MS-DOS. How advantageous is the usage?

It provides the capability of attaching several work stations to the PC, which then is no longer a "personal" computer. However, the load on the hardware increases significantly. In a normally configured AT compatible computer with 640K of main memory, XENIX would require almost half the available memory for itself permanently. If several users have to share the remaining memory space, the operating system must frequently load programs from the hard disk drive. Longer response times for the interactive operations are the net result.

It becomes inevitable that the amount of main memory must be increased significantly. This is possible since UNIX (or XENIX) is not limited to the 640K address space of MS-DOS. Furthermore a larger hard disk drive (60 MByte or more) should be used since UNIX, and the files created by it, require a large amount of disk storage.

In a computer which is not restricted by limited hardware, UNIX does offer a significant advantage over MS-DOS. A testimonial is the number of standard utility programs included with the operating system, over 200 with UNIX versus around 50 with MS-DOS.

The upward compatibility of the DOS versions, which resemble UNIX more and more even though based on CP/M, still limits the development capabilities of DOS significantly. Of the enhanced capabilities of the 80286 processor in the AT, only the higher speed is generally used.

The new OS/2 operating system from Microsoft opens the current border. The address space is 16 MBytes, and can even offer up to 1 GByte of virtual address space. OS/2 is mainly a multi-processing system. One of the programs can be an MS-DOS application which runs in a DOS compatibility box. Existing application programs can continue to be used and new programs can access the hardware, such as the display, directly.

Many OS/2 commands correspond to those of MS-DOS. Of course OS/2 is more powerful, and contains numerous additional commands which are partly related to the multi-processing capability. An example is the detach command which starts a background execution.

Some OS/2 features, such as the communication over pipes, are similar to those found in UNIX. Other OS/2 features are quite different from UNIX. In OS/2, its possible to bring any program executing in the background to the foreground. The commands currently input are then directed to the program executing in the foreground.

At this moment, OS/2 is not capable of multi-user operations. It does not represent a direct competition for UNIX, except for the single user variant XENIX. OS/2, in contrast with UNIX, is a processor dependent operating system for the INTEL 80286 and 80386 families.

UNIX is one of the most popular multi-user operating systems, regardless of the manufacturer and processor. Because of this, its viability is assured for years to come. In the professional area, an increased use of UNIX is predicted, and in fact is already starting to materialize. In the hobby market, the multi-user capability should remain a luxury for the foreseeable future. The sparse user interface will also meet resistance here. However, some effort is being made in this area to produce a manufacturer independent interface by the implementation of the X/WINDOW standard developed by the X/OPEN Group.

3. Overview of the UNIX operating system

This chapter contains a brief overview of the characteristics of UNIX, plus its history and future development are also presented.

3.1   Characteristics of UNIX

The success of UNIX is based on some of its characteristics. There are no roses without thorns and the disadvantages will not be neglected.

At this point characteristics are discussed under various headings. Additional information is provided in later chapters.

Portability

UNIX is an operating system which is independent of manufacturers and hardware. Normally operating systems are written in the assembler language of the processor and as a consequence can only be executed on a certain type of computer. If such an operating system should be transferred to another type of computer, only the concept, not the program itself, can be used.

Approximately 90% of UNIX was written in the C language. The C language is comparable with other higher level languages such as COBOL, Fortran or Pascal. It's very close to the hardware, but not machine dependent. Because of this, UNIX can be transported to any processor for which a C compiler exists. Only a small portion of the UNIX kernel (roughly 1,000 Assembler commands) must be rewritten.

The kernel contains, among other items, the drivers (device handlers) for the peripheral equipment. C was not well suited for this, since the language does not permit interrupt processing and does not handle bit manipulation easily.

Even greater portability can be achieved for the application programs if special capabilities of a certain UNIX derivative (see Section 3.3) are ignored.

Hierarchical file system

A UNIX file system consists of catalogs (file directories) and files. It is arranged like a tree and can be constructed by the user in a very visible manner. Chapter 5 describes this central concept in more detail.

Multi-user operation

UNIX is a multi-user and multi-processing system. Several users can work independently of each other on a computer using UNIX. At the same time, they can initiate several program executions. The assignment of a processor and various storage facilities are all handled by the operating system.

Security

Every user has a user and group identity associated with their user name used to log onto the system. Security passwords may also be utilized to protect access to the system or specific files and devices.

Files created by the user contain an identification to register ownership. Protection bits are stored for every UNIX file which regulate the access of the various user levels (owner, group of the owner, other users). Access rights are also differentiated for writing, reading and execution of any file or directory. More details about the various access rights appear in Section 5.7.

Command interpretation

The UNIX command interpreter is called a shell because it surrounds the operating system core like a shell. The kernel itself, in contrast with many other operating systems, has no interpreter. The shell is a normal application program and every user can use their own shell however desired.

There are several shells which are generally used on UNIX systems. The descriptions in this book are for the Bourne shell which provides a line oriented command interpreter. Various manufacturers offer alternative display screen oriented shells too (for example, the Menu shell for SINIX from Siemens).

The commands to be interpreted are program names, or names of executable files. The shell also has interpretative programming language capabilities with modern control structures (case, if... then... else, etc.). The shell is described in detail in Chapter 12.

Input and Output concept

The input and output media for UNIX is always files. If a program is started through the shell, the standard input, output and error files have already been opened. Files are referenced through a numerical file descriptor. For the three standard files these descriptors are 0, 1 and 2. These files are normally connected with the display terminal of the user (0 = keyboard, 1 & 2 = display). Every device is assigned at least one special file. If a peripheral device is addressed, the special file is read or written just like a normal file. An output to the display, magnetic tape or an ordinary file are all identical from a programming viewpoint. This opens the possibility of a simple redirection from the standard input and output to any other files or devices.

The shell interprets the less-than character "<" as a redirection of the standard input, and the greater-than character ">" as redirection for the standard output. More about redirection in Section 8.1.

Procedures

The execution of programs is described as a procedure. While a program is static, a procedure is dynamic. A procedure can terminate a program, eliminate the attached files and start a new program. A single program can generate and control several procedures which execute simultaneously.

The UNIX procedure structure is also like a tree. During system startup the root is generated. The second level grows for every user from the logon procedure as the shell or another program is started. The user has the opportunity to extend this process and to enhance the procedure hierarchy. More in Section 12.1.

Filter and pipelines

Programs which read from the standard input, process the data read in some manner and write to the standard output, are designated as filters. Filters offer the capability of redirecting the input or output from and to files on the shell level. The programs themselves cannot be changed.

A chaining of commands, or programs, in a command line is called a *pipeline*. These commands are started simultaneously by the shell. The chaining is done through nameless, temporary files, normally referred to as *pipes*. These conduct the output from one procedure to the input of the next procedure.

Utility programs

Besides the operating system kernel and the shell, UNIX contains more than 200 utility programs which can be input under their name as commands. They are used for file manipulation and processing, program execution, text processing, communication, program development, etc. Many of these utility programs have the characteristic of filters.

The central concept of UNIX is: "small is beautiful." Because of this the commands are short. A few examples follow:

cp	copy data
lp	output to the line printer
	(in some systems: lpr)
cc	call the C-compiler
rm	remove a file
cat	display files (catalog)

The experienced programmer appreciates the short names of the commands. More commands are covered in Chapters 6 and 9.

Disadvantages of UNIX

The advantage of short commands has the disadvantage of a higher learning requirement, since so many commands are difficult to remember. Only practice can help here.

More serious are two additional disadvantages:

- UNIX is disk and memory intensive. This is partially caused by the requirement that the minimum size of a file is 512 or 1,024 bytes, and storage of files occurs in blocks of 512 bytes. Also, many newer versions of UNIX use larger block sizes, such as in the Berkeley disk system with blocks of 4K each.

- The line oriented dialog at the Bourne shell level is not very user friendly.

Structural overview

The structure of UNIX can be illustrated with a block diagram.

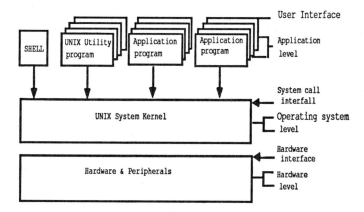

Figure 4

The kernel itself has the following main functions:

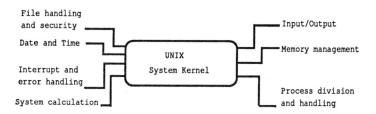

Figure 5

Summary

UNIX offers the following main advantages:

- Portability

- Standard operating system

- Application software

- Hierarchical file system

- Multi-user and multi-processing operation

- Shell concept

- Filter and pipelines

- Many utility programs

- Software development tools

The disadvantages are:

- Large memory and disk storage requirement

- Not user friendly at the shell level

3.2   History

The history of UNIX began in 1969 at Bell Laboratories, which is part of AT&T. Kenneth Thompson developed an operating system written in DEC PDP-7 assembler code for the "Space Travel" project. He called it UNIX. The name was derived from the preceding operating system Multics which was less conservative in the use of the scarce computer resources. UNIX was at first a single user variant of Multics.

In 1971 UNIX was implemented again in assembler code on the more powerful computers of the PDP-11 series. To become more independent from another change in hardware, Thompson planned a new implementation in a higher level language. He developed the B language from BCPL in 1970, but this language did not prove to be powerful enough.

After Dennis Ritchie, also at Bell, created the C language, UNIX was rewritten almost completely in this higher level language by 1973. By utilizing the advantages of C, UNIX became capable of handling multi-users and multi-tasking. UNIX was then machine independent and the start signal for its rapid distribution was given. At that time, Version 5 was still being distributed to American universities free of charge for use in research and education. Berkeley University in particular developed UNIX further. From this development came a unique branch of UNIX (see Figure 6).

The real triumph began in 1975 with Version 6. AT&T granted source licenses to interested companies, but without support. From this release, derivatives of UNIX were created which split away from the main development.

Version 7 of UNIX appeared about the same time as the first 16-bit microprocessors. This is the version on which most of todays UNIX derivatives are based. A third branch also developed, which is characterized most by the Microsoft product XENIX.

While UNIX was at first conceived for scientific and technical applications, XENIX also considered the commercial administrative requirements. Especially the access protection for files, with record locking, was improved considerably.

Since 1983 AT&T has tried to bring the various development streams together again. Training, documentation and other support is being offered. The external sign is a new number series known as System V.

Around the beginning of 1988, the third version (System V, release 3.0) was current. However, many producers were still using the previous release 2.0 version which already supported the virtual storage concept.

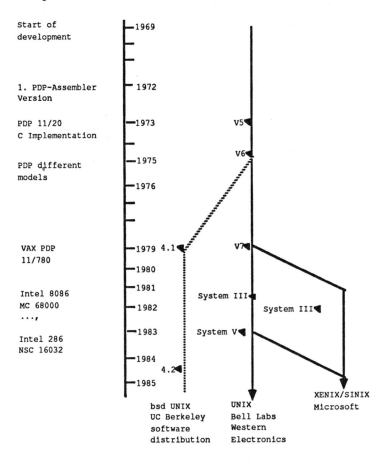

Figure 6

Limiting the number of UNIX derivatives is the main goal of users and many manufacturers, since the danger exists that the portability of UNIX can be lost. The European producers have formed the X/OPEN-Group for this reason. The following statement of purpose came from the 1984 committee report of the X/OPEN-Group's "Data Processing Regulations" from Westphalia.

X/OPEN-Group

The X/OPEN-Group was founded at the end of 1984 on the initiative of leading manufacturers of computer systems. The goal of this association was the promotion of the UNIX system for the following:

- To enlarge the number and quality of software products for the systems of its members.

- To insure the portability of software products on the source code level, to guard the investment of software manufacturers and to facilitate the sale of software.

The user of computer systems has the advantage of being able to compare systems from various manufacturers and to use mixed configurations. It makes the applications software from many producers available and the software developed for various applications will be available in the future on systems from other manufacturers.

A general applications environment will be defined by the X/OPEN-Group to help in achieving this goal. This specification will be based on the defined interfaces to the UNIX operating system as described in the AT&T System V Interface Definition.

Up to now agreement has been reached on:

- Programming languages (C, COBOL, Fortran, Pascal)
- Data management (C-ISAM, SQL)
- Data media (5" floppy disks and magnetic tape, 9 track, 1600 bpi)
- Security of the data
- Data exchange without media

Agreements on networks are planned on the basis of the ISO/OSI standards, for the Inter Process Communication, for distributed file systems and distributed processing for graphic applications (probably GKS), for additional programming languages and the source code transfer.

At this time seven European manufacturers (Bull, Ericsson, ICL, Nixdorf, Olivetti, Philips, and Siemens) and four American manufacturers (Digital Equipment, Unisys, HP, and AT&T) are members of the X/OPEN-Group.

A wider distribution of this new de-facto standard can be expected.

Concerning the development of UNIX itself, enhancements to System V 3.0 are now in progress. The networking capability will be improved significantly, mainly in the following areas:

- RFS (Remote File Sharing)

Aids the networking of UNIX computers and the common use of files and peripherals.

- STREAMS (a generalized network protocol framework)

The application programs remain unchanged when a network node changes protocol, or the network technology changes.

- Shared Libraries

The library elements are compiled object programs which are already allocated in storage. Only at the time of the execution of an application program are they dynamically linked. They must be present only once in main storage or on disk, which results in savings of storage space. If a library routine changes, the linking with all other programs which use it is not required. At run time, the latest version is automatically available.

- TLI (Transport Layer Interface)

Standardized interface of level 4 to the levels below in ISO/OSI-7 Level Reference Model, which can then be linked with STREAMS.

3.3   UNIX Portability

From the growing number of UNIX derivatives and systems similar to UNIX, some of the best known are listed here in alphabetical order. They contain, for example, enhancement and tailoring for special problems.

From the viewpoint of the "normal" user there is no reason for concern. The differences are usually less than reported. During applications which are machine dependent, some surprises may occur when a program is moved from one system to another. There is hope for improvement in connection with the X/OPEN-Group.

In the framework of this book the differences are even less significant.

System Name	Manufacturer or System House
Aix	IBM
bsd	University of California at Berkeley
Coherent	Mark Williams Co.
Cromix	Cromemco
Edition VII	Perkin-Elmer
EUNIX	Electronic Info System, Inc.
IDRIS	Whitesmith Ltd.
IS/1	Interactive Systems, Inc.
IS/5	Interactive Systems, Inc.
JOS	CRDS
MUNIX	PCS (Munich)
OS-1	Software Labs
SINIX	Siemens
Unica	Knowlogy
UTS	Amdahl (Large Computer implementation)
UNIX	Nixdorf
UX	Hewlett Packard
VENIX	Ventur Com Ulnc.
XENIX	Microsoft Co.
ZEUS	Zilog

Because of its hardware independence, UNIX is available on many computers of various manufacturers:

Altos	Digital Equipment	Perkin-Elmer
Amdahl	Fortune	Perq
Apollo	Forward	Philips
Apple	Four Phase	Pixel
AT&T	Gould	Plexus
Bolt Beranek	Hewlett Packard	Pyramid
Bull	IBM	Siemens
Burroughs	ICL	Sperry
Cadmus	Intel	Sun
Callan	Masscomp	Tandy
Charles River	Microbar	Tektronik
CIE Systems	Motorola	Televideo
Codata	National Semi	Valid Logic
Convergent	NCR	Wicat
Cromemco	Nixdorf	Zilog
Cosmos	Olivetti	
Data General	PCS	

To move UNIX to a new type of processor the following steps are required:

1.)   A C compiler must be written to permit translation of the C program package in UNIX into the machine language of the new processor.

2.)   The small hardware dependent portion of the system kernel, which is written in assembly language (about 1,000 instructions), must be rewritten.

3.)   The input/output drivers must be updated to handle the hardware of the input/output devices used.

This effort is substantially less than required for an operating system written in Assembler. The reduced amount of work allows even smaller producers to solve the portability problem which favors wider distribution of UNIX.

The "small" operators do not have the opportunity to join the X/OPEN-Group because of the requirement for sales of at least $500 million. However, they can at least adhere to the published recommendations of X/OPEN to provide compatible systems.

4. Talking with UNIX

UNIX is a dialogue-oriented operating system. This chapter begins to describe some of the basic techniques in communicating with UNIX.

A new user

A UNIX computer configuration is one managed by a super-user. The system administrator's tasks are outlined in Chapter 14. Before you can work with the computer, the super-user must make some preparatory steps:

- Define the user name

- Assign the logon password (optional)

- Create and define the home directory (assigned as the user's main directory in the UNIX file tree)

- Establish the user group assignment

System Initialization

In a large, multi-user system, the user does not have to perform the system startup, the system operator will usually take care of this task. In smaller systems, the system startup is usually very simple. With many systems, the procedure may be as simple as just turning on the system and letting it initialize itself. Check the documentation for your particular system if you should need to handle the initialization yourself.

Once you have a working system, you should see a prompt for a valid `"user-id"` and password on your display terminal. After successful input, the shell displays a `"$"` (or `"#"` for the super-user). If a system error occurs, a message may be displayed on the system console.

Keyboard Assignment
for the Interactive Terminal

UNIX is a line oriented system at the Bourne shell level. There is no Block mode, but there are some special keys to correct input and influence the programs which are running. These are described in the following table.

Special keys

Alternate key combinations supported by most systems:

Keys	Reaction
<Ctrl><H>	Erase character <Backspace>
<Ctrl><X>	Erase line
<Ctrl><D>	End of File (EOF), terminate shell <logoff>
<Ctrl><S>	Suspend display
<Ctrl><Q>	Continue display
<Ctrl><C>	Terminate program <del>
<Ctrl><\>	Terminate program with DUMP
<Ctrl><G>	Bell
<CR>	End of command input (carriage return)

The Control key sequences indicated above are entered by simultaneous activation of the indicated key with the Control key.

Become familiar with the manual for the particular system you are using. If necessary, a user familiar with the system can be consulted about control keys particular to your system. Be aware that the key assignments can be changed with the parameters of the UNIX stty command.

The shell as a command interpreter

After the user has signed on the system, the shell takes over the function of intermediary between the user and the UNIX kernel. The dialog proceeds as follows:

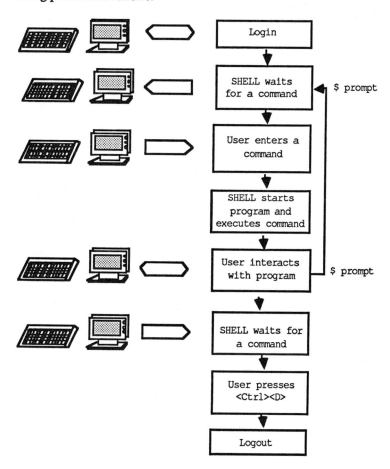

Figure 7

The dialog with UNIX consists mainly of input commands, which trigger certain actions or which can lead to prompts for input of additional information.

Commands are entered on the current display line following the shell prompt (i.e. "$"). They consist of one or more words, where a word is a continuous character chain up to the next blank. The first word entered indicates the appropriate command or program name to be executed. All following words represent parameters that are passed to the program.

There are two kinds of parameters:

1.) Normal parameters, such as input or output files which the called program should use.

2.) Options and additional information which influence the execution of the program. Without options specified, a default execution is always standard. Program options then allow selectable variations specific to an executing program. Options are always designated with a preceding minus character (−) to differentiate them from the normal parameters (file names).

The complete syntax of a command is as follows:

```
command_name [option ...] [argument ...]
```

All inputs are terminated with a carriage return <CR>. UNIX commands are case sensitive and are usually lowercase letters. Uppercase letters may create error conditions!

Exercises

1.) Sign on at the terminal by entering the user-ID at the system logon prompt. If necessary, ask the super-user for a valid user-ID.

Enter the appropriate password corresponding to the user-ID in use. After completion of the opening procedure, the shell will respond with the "$" prompt.

2.) The `passwd` command allows changing a user's login password. Try inputting the `passwd` command, then enter a new password. Remember it well!

The password should be longer than 6 characters or the system will reject it. On systems with UNIX V.2 or later, passwords must consist of numbers and letters unless entered by the super-user.

If the password is acceptable, the system will ask you to repeat it. The login password will only be changed after the entered password is confirmed. If a user forgets their password, the super-user can help.

3.) Input the `who` command. A list of all current users, including device names and login time will be provided on the standard output device (your display terminal).

4.) Test the mechanism of the output redirection.

Try inputting: `who >whodat`

The output is sent to the `whodat` file. List this file on the display with the `cat whodat` command.

5.) Count the number of lines, words and characters in `whodat` by entering: `wc whodat`.

6.) Use the pipe mechanism for simplification.

Input: `who | wc`

The intermediate file storage `whodat` is not used.

7.) Sign off the system by pressing <Ctrl><D> or inputting the exit command.

Remember that all commands must be input in lowercase letters. This is significant. Uppercase letters will more than likely produce error messages.

Repeat the sign-on procedure and then try the following command.

8.) Input: who

For every active user, a line is displayed with the following information: User number, login display, and login time.

9.) Input the following commands, one at a time:

```
who am I
who X Y
who X
WHO X Y
woh X Y
```

Observe the reaction of the system for each command entered.

10.) Input: ls -l /bin

List a line in "longform" (option -l) for every file in the directory /bin.

11.) Input: ls /bin

Only the filenames are displayed.

12.) Input: date

The system returns the current time and date.

13.) Input: cal 11 1986

The system returns the calendar display for the month of November 1986.

14.) Input: `cal 1986`

Outputs calendar displays for every month in the year 1986. The output is several pages long, so try the following operations while it's being dislayed:

Suspend the output:	<Ctrl><S>
Continue the output:	<Ctrl><Q>
Interrupt the running program:	<Ctrl><C>
Terminate the session:	<Ctrl><D>

These exercises were a jump into cold water. If everything was not perfectly clear, don't be concerned. At this time it is only important to begin to become familiar with the system. However, it will be helpful later if you practice the use of the special keys outlined in this chapter.

User Communication

Several commands are available for users to communicate with both active and inactive users.

write   Send message to an active user.

mesg   Permit or deny spontaneous messages.

mail   Deposit message for a user in the mailbox, or read message in the mailbox.

Send Message (WRITE)

Syntax: write user-id

Several text lines can be input, with each line terminated with a <CR>. End the message by pressing <Ctrl><D> at the beginning of a line.

Each line of a message is transmitted after every <CR> is entered allowing a dialog to be sent.

Example: write u2

              ...text

              <Ctrl><D>

Permit/deny Message (MESG)

Syntax: mesg [y] [n]

mesg y   Messages are allowed from now on (default).

mesg n   Messages are denied from now on (until mesg y is entered or the end of the session). This is important and useful while working with the editor, otherwise the text input could be destroyed by a message.

mesg   The command entered without a parameter will indicate whether or not messages are currently permitted.

Fill and Empty Mailbox (MAIL)

Syntax: `mail [options] [use-ID]`

`mail user-ID`

Sends a message to the mailbox of a user. No indication appears on the screen of the user.

Example: `mail u3`

Send the message as in the `write` command and terminate with <Ctrl><D> or <CR> on a new line.

After the next login, the user u3 gets the message "You have mail" or something similar from the system.

`mail [option]`

Reads the mailbox and if necessary processes the message.

The mail is normally read in reverse order of entry: Last in, first out.

Options:	`-r`	Read in sequence of input
	`-f file`	File is used as mail drop

Other options exist.

The system outputs a message and expects input from the user:

Input	Action
<CR>	Shows next message, do not erase old message
<q> or	Quit or
<Ctrl><D>	exit Mail command
d	Erases old message, displays next message
s file	Stores message in indicated file otherwise as in d. The message header is also included.
w file	File as in s, but without the message header.
m user-id	Send message to the indicated user
p	Output of the message is repeated

The following illustration explains the use of the `mail` command:

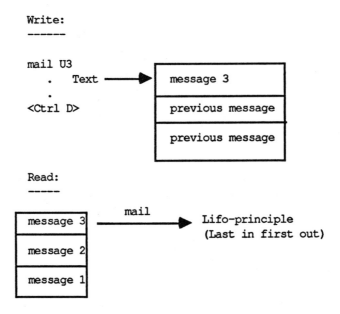

```
Write:
------

mail U3
      .    Text  ──────▶  message 3
      .                   previous message
<Ctrl D>                  previous message


Read:
-----
                   mail
message 3  ────────────────▶  Lifo-principle
message 2                     (Last in first out)
message 1
```

Figure 8

Note that the system can also send its own messages. The most common is difficulty with a printer.

Exercises

1.)   Conduct a dialog with another user.

2.)   Prohibit further write-messages and send a write-message to yourself. Then permit messages again and send another message to yourself.

3.)   Send a mail message to yourself and, if necessary, perform another login to see the message indicating that mail has arrived. Read the message.

4.)   Send mail messages to other users.

5.)   Read the mailbox and try some options.

6.)   Empty the mailbox.

5. File Systems

The file system is of central significance. An in-depth examination is needed to understand this system. From the user's viewpoint there are four types of files in UNIX:

- Ordinary files

- Directories

- Special files (device files):
  - Block oriented
  - Character oriented

- Named pipes

An ordinary file corresponds to conventional files which are familiar from other operating systems. They can contain programs, data sets or text. UNIX does not recognize structural characteristics such as sets, blocks, sectors, etc. -- only structureless byte chains. Special forms of storage (for example ISAM) are handled by application programs.

Directories

Directories handle the linking of filenames to files. Every user has at least one directory and can have any number. Directories can be read by anyone with access, but can only be changed by the system. If the user has access permission, the working directory can be relocated to any desired place in the file hierarchy.

Special files are assigned to peripheral devices. The mechanism of data transfer between programs and ordinary files does not differ from the transfer between programs and device files. File and device names have the same syntax and significance. Also, the protection mechanism for peripherals does not differ from those for ordinary files (see below).

The fourth file type (called pipes) will not be discussed in further detail.

The structure of the UNIX file system is hierarchical (like a tree). Originating in a root, the directories correspond to branch nodes. The ordinary and special files correspond to the leaves on a tree.

The following illustration should demonstrate this concept. The tree is shown upside down (root on top). The file system can also be compared to an organizational chart.

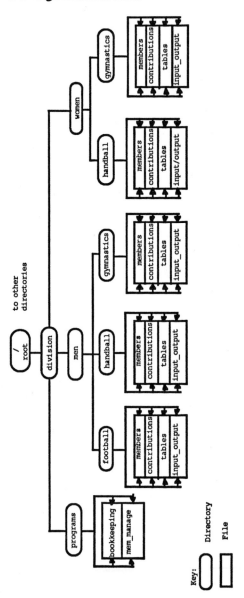

Figure 9

5.1   Filenames

Filenames can normally be up to 14 characters long, while some UNIX implementations like Berkeley may allow longer filenames. All characters are permitted. Usually only the alphanumeric and the special characters " . " (period) and "_" (underline) are used. Many UNIX systems use conventions for filename extensions.

Examples:

> .o   for object files
>
> .c   for C source programs

Extensions do not have basic significance as in DOS.

Basically a file can only be addressed through the pathname. It can be indicated either absolute or relative. Absolute means "from the root up", and is designated with a starting slash (/) in the pathname.

Pathnames

The complete access path reaches from the root to the desired file. All directories along this path must be indicated in the pathname. The individual directory names must be separated with a slash (/).

The relative pathname is related to the working directory which is the current directory (see below). As the last illustration shows, a filename doesn't have to be unique. It can occur several times in a file hierarchy. The filename "tables" has been used a total of 5 times. It becomes unique only through the pathname. The same is true of the directories (for example 'handball').

For example, in the membership file for the department "Football" the absolute pathname is:

> /division/men/football/members

Assume that at this moment the user wants to work only with the department "Football". To avoid entering the complete pathname, the working directory is set to /division/men.

The desired file is now reached with the input football/members. This pathname is relative to the current working directory

/division/men. It is automatically augmented with the absolute pathnames by the operating system.

| absolute pathname | always begins with / (root) |
| relative pathname | begins without / |

There are three possibilities to reach a current directory (working directory):

1.) In the password file of every user is a login directory which automatically becomes the working directory after every login. The login directory is determined by the super-user.

2.) The working directory can be changed with the cd (change directory) command.

Example: cd /division/women/handball

changes the access path in such a manner that the input command addresses the proper file (see Fig. 9).

3.) The cd command without additions changes the working directory to the home directory. The name of the home directory is stored in the shell variable HOME and can be changed by the user at any time. The shell variables are discussed in greater detail in Chapter 9.

Those familiar with MS-DOS, will recognize the concept of pathnames. The only difference is that the backslash (\) is used in DOS in place of the slash (/) used in UNIX.

5.2   Directories

It's important to understand that three concepts are used synonymously.

> File directory = Catalog = Directory

A file directory contains pointers to other files, mainly two:

*   One to itself.

*   One to the higher level parent directory. This corresponds to the next level in the direction of the root.

A directory which only contains these two pointers is called an empty file directory.

Example: Parent directory for `gymnastics` is `men`.

Instead of the parent, a double period "`..`" is entered, instead of its own name a single period "`.`" is entered. The command `cd ..` creates a change to the higher level directory.

Example:
Working directory is:

>   `/division/men/handball`

After input of: `cd ..`

Working directory is:

>   `/division/men`.

The following indicators are used in connection with directories:

>   `/`   Root directory

>   `..`   Parent directory

>   `.`   Working directory

The entry of a file into a directory consists of the node number or the i-node-number of the file as well as the filename.

Every file system has a table of contents containing all of the files in the system. This table is called the i-node or file header list. The i-node-number is an index (pointer to an entry) in the i-node-list. This is true for all file oriented structures on a single, logical data medium with random access, such as a hard disk drive.

During creation of a file, a new i-node (file header) is created. The name and index of the file are then entered into the proper directory. A file does not have to be uniquely assigned to one directory. For example, two directories can point to the same file.

Figure 10-1

The name of the file in v1 and v2 can be completely different. In any case, the i-node-number is identical. The elements of the i-node-list are the "i-nodes" which are generated during the creation of a file.

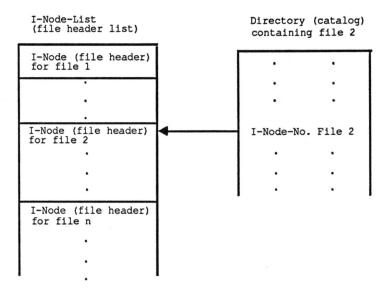

Figure 10-2

An i-node (File Header) contains the following information:

File type:	**.**	=	normal file
	d	=	directory
	b	=	device file, block oriented
	c	=	device file, character oriented
	p	=	named pipe (Fifo)

access right:	**r**	=	read
	w	=	write
	x	=	(program) execute

Number of references to file
Owner (UID)
Group (GID)
Length in bytes
Pointers to the data blocks within the file
Time of last access of the file
Time of last modification of the file
Time of creation of the file (change of i-nodes)

The further significance of some of these entries will be explained later. Information about most of these entries can be obtained with the ls command which has been encountered in the exercises, but will be described in more detail later.

5.3   Important Directories in UNIX

A UNIX file tree normally begins as in the following illustration:

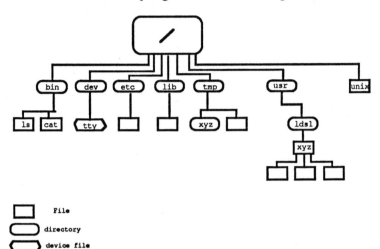

Figure 11

Some important directories in the "root" area of the UNIX file tree are described briefly below.

The directories are created during the installation of the system.

Contents of the system specific directories:

/	"root directory"
/bin	most UNIX commands
/dev	device files
/etc	commands for the super-user and system files
/include	"include files" for C programs
/lib	general object library
/lost+found	used by /etc/fsck for restoration of files
/tmp	temporary files which are normally erased during every boot
/usr	user and installation specific files
/usr/lib	installation specific object libraries
/usr/tmp	temporary files normally erased during every boot
/usr/include	installation specific "include files" (used in several programs)

5.4   Normal Files

Normal files in /etc (super-user files)

checklist	Used to check file system
group	User groups
motd	Super-user file with the "message of the day"
mtab	Table of mounted file systems
passwd	Passwords for system users
termcap	Characteristics of the displays
utmp	List of current users (who)
rc	Shell procedure which runs at every boot

/ETC/PASSWD

Every user is registered in this file. The following examples show a complete user entry in the file /etc/passwd. Every field on a line must be separated with a colon (:) and there is one line for every user.

        u2:A7urtB9a:4:2:Tom Mix:/usr/u2:/bin/sh

The entries mean:

u2	User name for login
A7urtB9a	Coded password (can be missing)
4	User identification, UID
2	Group identification, GID
Tom Mix	Remarks, typically the full user name
/usr/u2	Login working directory
/bin/sh	Program to be executed after login (If no indication, the shell is started automatically). May be a special program if required.

It is customary to give every user a login file directory /usr/user-number, for example /usr/u2. User entries are managed by the super-user using the editor. Some systems offer super-user tools and may organize the disk differently.

/ETC/GROUP

The following example shows a complete user entry in the file
/etc/group. Every field on a line must be separated with a colon
(:) and a line exists for every group.

```
g1:x79Brkz:6:u1,u2,u3
```

The entries mean:

g1	Name of the group
x79Brkz	Coded password (usually missing)
6	Group identification, GID
u1,u2,u3	Names of users permitted to work in this group

There is no UNIX command to create a password for a group. With the
editor, you can copy a coded password which is known in decoded form
from the passwd file.

.profile

Every user can create a file named .profile in their default working
directory. This file normally contains opening procedures which execute
after every logon under your user-ID. Later exercises will return to this
concept.

Example: /usr/u2/.profile

The .profile file is comparable in its actions with the
AUTOEXEC.BAT file used by MS-DOS.

5.5   Device Files

There are special files for the physical devices which are addressed with their corresponding filename. For the user, there is no difference between input or output to or from files and devices. This makes the principle of input/output redirection with greater-than ">" and less-than "<" characters very easy as discussed later in Section 8.1. Device files are usually in the /dev directory. Some examples follow:

Pseudo devices

/dev/console	System console (printer or terminal), where system messages are displayed.
/dev/null	Null device: Every output to it is thrown away and every input results only in an End Of File (EOF). This is generally used for test purposes.

Real devices

/dev/lp	Printer
/dev/mtn	Manetic tape, unit number n
/dev/nmtn	As above, but no automatic rewind after every closing of the file.
/dev/ttyn	Dialog station (display terminal), number n
/dev/hkn	Hard disk drive, number n

Character and block oriented devices (device files) are identified. Display terminals and printers are character oriented devices, while magnetic tape units, hard disks and floppies are block oriented.

The device files will not be discussed further in this introduction, but redirection of input to a device file should be practiced.

If a nearby terminal is accessible under the device file tty03, try inputting:

```
cat  /etc/passwd  >/dev/tty03
```

What happens?

5.6   Physical Structure of the File System

A physical UNIX file system consists of blocks 512 bytes long or some multiple of 512 bytes, such as 1,024 bytes. The blocks are numbered in ascending order, starting from zero. They have the following construction:

Block 0	Boot Block
Block 1	Super-Block
Block 2	First file header
Block 3	. file header list . (I-node list)
Block n	nth file header
Block N+1	Data blocks
Block m	

Figure 12

The basic loader is a short machine language program which is activated during the start of UNIX. It loads a file and executes it without requiring the support of the operating system, which has not yet been loaded. The second block (block Nr. 1) is the Superblock, which keeps all the information necessary for use of the file system available.

This information is as follows:

- Size of the file system in blocks

- Name of the logical data carrier (label)

- Size of the file header list (i-node-list)

- Pointer to the list of the available data blocks

- Pointer to the list of the available i-nodes

- Date of the last modification

- Date of the last storage

- Indicator for blocking data access

- Indicator for 512 or 1,024 byte blocks (larger block sizes are now in use on some systems)

Block 2 begins with the first file header of the file header list (i-node-list) which was described in Section 5.2. The same is true for some entries in the file header (see Section 5.2). The pointers to data blocks and redirection are interesting. The first 10 pointers point to the first 10 blocks of the file. (If the file is smaller, there are fewer pointers). Physically the pointers are block numbers (addresses). Since the block represents the smallest addressable unit, the minimum size of a UNIX file is the size of one disk block, independent of the file type.

If the file is larger than 10 blocks, up to three indirections can be used. While the first 10 references are direct, the first indirection points to a block which contains up to 128 further references. The second indirection points to a block with 128 indirect references of the first level. If necessary, the third indirection contains 128 references to indirect references of the second step.

Assuming a block size of 512 bytes, the maximum size of a UNIX file therefore is:

$$
\begin{array}{rcr}
10 \times 512 & = & 5{,}120 \text{ bytes} \\
+\ 128 \times 512 & = & 65{,}536 \text{ bytes} \\
+\ 128 \times 128 \times 512 & = & 8{,}388{,}608 \text{ bytes} \\
\underline{+\ 128 \times 128 \times 128 \times 512} & \underline{=} & \underline{1{,}073{,}741{,}824 \text{ bytes}} \\
& & 1{,}082{,}201{,}088 \text{ bytes}
\end{array}
$$

That's one GigaByte!

In reality, the maximum file size is limited by the disk capacity. The number of files is not limited by the disk capacity, but by the maximum number of i-nodes (file headers) in the i-node-list.

The following illustration demonstrates the UNIX reference structure:

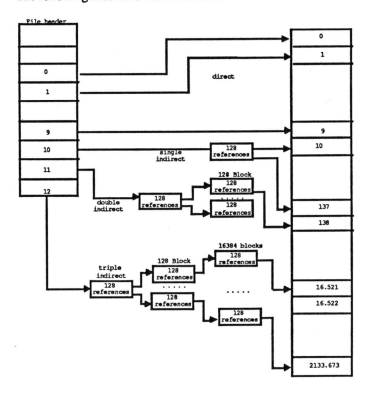

Figure 13

Since access to the first 10 blocks is direct, the access time is correspondingly short. As the number of indirect references increases, so does the number of required disk accesses to reach the desired file block. The access time grows so that the UNIX motto "small is beautiful" retains its validity.

5.7   Access Rights and Protection

The file owner is normally the user who created the file. He can determine the access rights of the file and change them at any time. The following command is used: chmod

UNIX permits three access rights:

    r   read

    w   write

    x   execute

These rights can be assigned to three user classes:

    u   owner of the file (user)

    g   group of the owner (group)

    o   all other users (other)

The three user categories are gathered together under the term "All", meaning universal access for all system users.

The right to execute (x) is the weakest. It makes sense if the file contains an executable program. In directories, the x-right indicates that access is permitted to directories and files which are deeper inside the structure.

Read (r) privileges allow the authorized user to view the file without changing it. In the case of a directory, the r-right is required for viewing the table of contents.

The right to write (w) makes it possible to change files. Those who can write to the directory, can erase the files listed in that directory.

A user group consists of all the users with the same group number as established in the /etc/group file.

A user can only belong to one group. The working user group can be changed with the newgrp command. Access rights can be determined with the ls command. Since the access rights are recorded in the file header (i-node), they exist only once even if several pointers exist to the file, or if the file is listed under several names.

During the creation of a file, the following standard access rights are typically assigned:

```
user   group   other
rwx     r-x     r-x
```

The standard setting can be changed with the umask command.

Exercises

1.) When is a UNIX file completely erased?

2.) What happens under UNIX during access to a file (three essential steps)?

3.) A section of a UNIX file system has the following appearance:

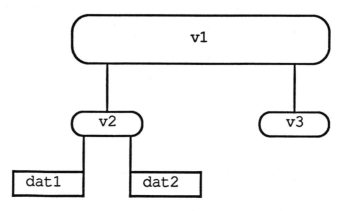

Figure 14

The current file directory is sequentially:

    a) v2

    b) v1

    c) v3

You want to access file dat2. What relative name must be given? Use the alternative ".." and "." formats.

Solutions

1.) When the number of pointers to this file is zero.

2.) Step One: Search for the i-node-number of the filename in the catalog.

   Step Two: Access the i-node (file header) through the i-node-number. Test the characteristics (for example access rights). Access can be permitted or denied.

   Step Three: Through the direct or indirect references in the file header physically access the file by blocks.

3.) a) dat2   or   ./dat2
     b) v2/dat2   or   ./v2/dat2
     c) ../v2/dat2   or   ./../v2/dat2

   Why not v1/v2/dat2 ?

6. UNIX Commands

In UNIX there is no difference between a command and a (user) program. Both are executed after the input of their name.

UNIX is a line-oriented operating system (on the Bourne shell level). Commands must be input one line after another and are executed in the order entered. When the same command is to be executed twice, it must be entered twice. The cursor keys are ignored by the command interpreter (shell). There is normally no repeat function key like that provided by the F3 key in MS-DOS. Individual commands are always treated in the same manner.

The following sections describe the most important UNIX commands. Special commands used in connection with procedures are also discussed.

Within each description, items enclosed in brackets "[..]" are optional. The corresponding MS-DOS command is presented, if it exists. The formal description is kept as short as possible. Examples are presented to help explain the most important applications of these commands. To become familiar with them, use these examples and refer to the documentation that was included with your system.

6.1   File oriented Commands

In Chapter 5, the file system theory was discussed. The commands described next are used to deliver information about files and permit the user to arrange the file system to his needs.

LS

Syntax: `ls [option] [directory] [...]`

Function: Returns the table of contents of the directory or the file indicated. If no directory is specified, it defaults to the current working directory.

Options: -a   All entries, even files which begin with a period (.) are shown.

             -d   If the file is a directory, its name but not its table of contents is output.

             -i   Outputs the i-node-number in the first column of the list.

             -l   Long or extended format (see example).

             -s   File size in blocks is output.

                     Many other options exist.

MS-DOS: `dir [directory] [/options]`

Example: `ls   -l`

For every file a line is output in long format:

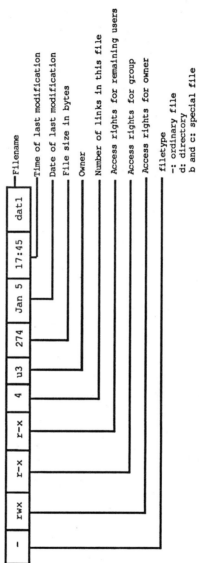

Figure 15

In UNIX V.2 and later systems, the group is displayed behind the owner.

CD

Syntax:	`cd [directory]`
Function:	Changes the working directory to the specified directory.
Options:	None
Comment:	Without a parameter, the home directory becomes the working directory (stored in the shell variable $HOME).
MS-DOS:	`chdir directory` or: `cd directory`

Examples:

cd .   nothing changes

cd /   root becomes the working directory (wd)

cd ..   parent directory becomes wd

cd ../equal
        the directory equal in the parent directory becomes wd

cd /division/women/handball
        the directory indicated (complete pathname) becomes wd

PWD

Syntax:	pwd
Function:	Indicates the name of the current working directory (complete pathname).
Options:	None
MS-DOS:	chdir or: cd
Example:	

    pwd   The name of the current working directory is displayed on the screen.

MKDIR

Syntax:	`mkdir directory1 [directory2] ...`
Function:	Creates one or more directories.
Options:	None
Comment:	The standard access rights are given (see `chmod`). Owner is the creator.
MS-DOS:	`mkdir directory` or: `md directory`

Examples:

    mkdir /usr/u2/c
The named, complete pathname directory is created.

    mkdir opa oma
The directories opa and oma are created within the current working directory.

RMDIR

Syntax:	`rmdir directory1 [directory2] ...`
Function:	Removes the indicated, empty directories (see `rm` command).
Options:	None
Comment:	Only the owner and super-user are permitted to use this command. In principle, any user can remove a directory if they have write permission to the higher level directory.
MS-DOS:	`rmdir directory` or: `rd directory`
Example:	

    `rmdir /usr/u3`
    Remove the login directory of user u3
    (only the super-user can do this).

    `rmdir cprog`
    Remove the `cprog` directory in the current working
    directory.

RM

Syntax:	`rm [options] file1 [file2] ...`

Function: 1.)   Erases all indicated files.
            2.)   Also erases directories which do not need to be empty (see option −r).

Options: −f   Erases the files indicated, even if write protected, without questioning the user.

            −i   Before the file is erased, the user is asked if erasing should actually occur. Erases only if the response is y.

            −r   Allows specifying directories. The references in the directory are erased recursively and finally the directory itself. Provides an opportunity to erase directories which are not empty.

MS-DOS: `delete  file`
            `del     file`
            `erase   file`

Comment: If the −f option was not used the system will inquire each time it encounters a write protected file. Any user who has write authorization for a directory can erase it.

Examples:

`rm   dat`

Assuming `dat` is a normal file, it's erased from the current directory, but may still exist in another directory (see Fig.16 and the `ln` command).

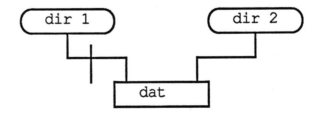

Figure 16

rm -i /usr/u1/*
>Erases all files in /usr/u1 interactively (option -i).
>The * represents any desired character chain. In this case
>any filename. The exact meaning of * is explained in
>Chapter 7.

rm -rf test
>Erases the files in test, and then the directory test
>itself, without checking with the user.

LN

Syntax: 1.)   ln old new
             2.)   ln dat1 [dat2] [•••] dir
                     (see cp command discussed next)

Function: Gives the indicated file an additional (Alias) name
             through which it can be addressed, or connects the file
             to an additional directory (Link).

Options: -f   Command is executed without checking with
                     the user, even if the file old is write
                     protected.

Comment: The ln command cannot be used with directories, only
             with files. The ln command creates an Alias name in
             the same directory, or breaks through the hierarchical
             system (a leaf is attached to several branches). If the file
             dat (see Fig. 17) should be erased later, this must
             occur in both directories to make the erasure complete.

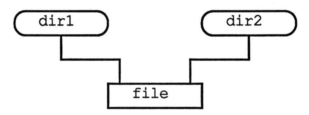

Figure 17

MS-DOS: Aliases and file links are not supported.

Examples:

      ln   otto   karl
             Creates an Alias name in the same working directory.
             The file otto is now accessible under karl.

      ln   /bin/pwd   /usr/u3/wd
             The UNIX pwd command is now executable with wd
             (under /usr/u3).

      ln   /dir1/dat   /dir2/dat
             Creates the condition shown in the Figure 17.

CP

Syntax: 1.)   `cp file1 file2`
            2.)   `cp dat1 [dat2] [...] ... dir`

Function: 1.)   Copies `file1` to `file2`. If `file2` already
                   exists, the old content is erased but the
                   attributes remain.
            2.)   If the last name is a directory, all files
                   indicated are copied into this directory.

Options: None

MS-DOS: `copy file1 file2`

Examples:

    cp   d1   d2
        Copies file d1 into file d2, both in the working
        directory.

    cp   /usr/project1/a1   /usr/save/a1
        Copies the file a1 to a different directory under /usr.

    cp   a   b   c   d   save
        Copies four files from the current working directory to
        the save directory. Write authorization must exist for
        the save directory.

Exercises:

The commands learned so far permit the user to perform demanding tasks. Practice these commands so you are sure you have a complete understanding of them.

The organization chart in Figure 9 is used for the following exercises. Create the partial tree (Fig.9) starting with the men directory, not from the root as indicated by the figure. Use cd to examine various branches of the tree and check with pwd.

A normal file can be created as follows:

```
cat  >tables
abc
<Ctrl><D>
```

The tables file (relative to the working directory) would then have the content abc. However, the content isn't important in the framework of this assignment.

MV

Syntax: 1.)   `mv nam1 nam2`
             2.)   `mv nam1 [nam2] [...] ... dir`

Function: 1.)   File `nam1` is renamed as `nam2`.
             2.)   The pointers to the files are erased and entered
                      in the directory indicated, moving the files to
                      the new directory.

Options: `-f`   The command is executed without asking the
                      user, even if the file is write protected.

MS-DOS: `rename nam1 nam2` or: `ren nam1 nam2`

Examples:

   `mv f-old f-new`
      The file `f-old` gets the `f-new` name in the same
      directory.

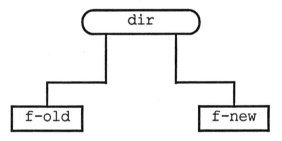

Figure 18.1

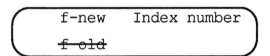

Figure 18.2

   `mv f-old /usr/u3`
      Erases the `f-old` file in the working directory and
      creates a new entry (for `f-old`) in the `/usr/u3`
      directory.

CHMOD

Syntax: 1.)   chmod XXX file1 [...]
             2.)   chmod [ugoa] [+-=] [rwx] file1 [...]
             3.)   chmod [ugoa]=[ugo] file1 [...]

Function: Changes the access rights of the indicated files.

Remarks:
For 1)   XXX stands for 3 octal numbers, which are calculated
             from the addition of the following:

400	Right to read	for the owner
200	Right to write	for the owner
100	Right to execute	for the owner
40	Right to read	for the group
20	Right to write	for the group
10	Right to execute	for the group
4	Right to read	for all other users
2	Right to write	for all other users
1	Right to execute	for all other users

Added properly, a 3 place octal number is obtained
(with digits of 0 to 7), which completely describe the
access rights (see example for 1).

For 2)   Symbolic format for setting rights:

             [ugoa] indicates user class (any combination):
                       u   User
                       g   Group
                       o   All others
                       a   All user classes

             [+-=] indicates an operation:
                       +   Right given
                       -        Right denied
                       =   Set right

             [rwx] indicates permission (any combination):
                       r   Right to read
                       w   Right to write
                       x   Right to execute

for 3)   The left user class is assigned the same rights as the right user class.

Some other access rights or priviledges exist which are not important in the framework of this introduction. With the help of examples, the three forms of setting access rights will be illustrated.

MS-DOS: No differentiated access rights since it is a single user system.

Examples:

for 1)   chmod   751   info
              access rights for the file are assigned as follows: rwx
              r-x   --x.

              Meaning that the user has full access rights while users in the same group can only read and execute, but all other users can only execute.

for 2)   chmod   g+w   info
              Write access is added for group members.

              chmod   o-x   info
                  Execute access is removed for all other users.

              chmod   g=rx   info
                  Group members can only read and execute.

for 3)   chmod   a=u   info
              All users can do everything that is permitted to the user.

Comments:
   1.)   Only the user of a file or the super-user can change the access rights (the Mode). In principle, everyone who has write access to a directory can change write access.

   2.)   The following table is for the octal version of chmod:

	u	g	o
r	400	40	4
w	200	20	2
x	100	10	1

FIND

Syntax:
```
find dir1 [...] condition1 [...] action1 [...]
```

Function: Searches the file hierarchy, starting at the directories indicated, for certain criteria and if necessary performs certain actions on the file which are found. If no condition is given, a hit is always assumed.

Conditions:

-atime n	File last accessed n days ago (Sign of n as in -size below)
-group name	Files belonging to the specified group
-inum n	Files with the index number n (Sign of n as in -size below)
-links n	Files with n pointers
-mtime n	Files changed in the last n days (Sign as in -size below)
-name file	Files with matching filenames
-newer file	Files which are newer than those indicated (very useful for backup functions)
-perm xxx	Files with specific access right xxx (for example 751)
-perm -xxx	Files with access right of at least xxx
-size n	Files of n blocks in size, where the sign of the n parameter means:

(space)	Equal to
-n	Smaller than
+n	Larger than

type f	Files of the specified type, where the file type is indicated by:

b	Device file block oriented
c	Device file character oriented
d	Directory
f	Normal File

-user name	files belonging to the specified user.

Other options also exist.

Options which initiate actions include:

-print	Output the file found (Access path). Can return a value of significance for shell procedures: 0 = true 1 = false

-exec cmd	Shell commands are executed if conditions are true (Return value = 0). Terminate the command list with the backslash character "\". In the command string, braces { } are replaced with the access path.

-ok cmd	As in exec, but provides an interactive test before each command is executed. The command is only executed after entering a yes/no response (y/n).

MS-DOS:	Not included in standard DOS command set, but similar utilities are available.
Remarks:	Several conditions can follow each other. The sequence of the options is important as they are evaluated from left to right. If conditions follow each other, they must all be true. Several operators allow combining conditions as required:

-a	permits a logical AND
-o	permits a logical OR
!	means negation (NOT)

Examples:

```
find  /usr/u3  -name  "pr*"  -print
```
Finds files whose name start with pr and are located in branches starting with /usr/u3. All filenames found are output.

```
find  /usr/u3/cprog  -name  "*.c"  -exec rm {} \;
```
Erases all C source programs (files with the .c suffix) starting at directory /usr/u3/cprog.

```
find  .  -mtime  +30  -exec  rm  {}  \
```
Erases all files which were changed more than 30 days ago, starting at the current directory.

```
rm  -i  `find  .  -mtime  +30  -print`
```
Similar action but interactive erasing after output of the filename. The exact meaning of the escape symbols (` `) is explained later (shell quoting).

```
find  /usr  -type  d  -print
```
Finds and outputs all directories occurring after the /usr directory.

```
find  .  -perm  755  -o  -user  u3  -print
```
Outputs all files, starting at the current directory, which have the access right 755, or which belong to user u3.

```
find  /usr  -user  u3  -ok  rm  {}  \;
```
Erases all files of user u3 interactively when the prompt is answered with y.

Please note that the find command requires that a starting directory be indicated immediately after the command name. If the starting directory is the current working directory, a period (.) must be used.

7. Wildcards

The wildcard concept comes from card playing.

Wildcard replacements are common in many operating systems including MS-DOS and UNIX. In both systems, special characters can represent any character or character string in the corresponding position. MS-DOS, however, only recognizes the question mark (?) and asterisk (*) wildcards.

With a single command, the shell can perform the desired action on several files using wildcards. For example: `rm  *` removes all files in the current directory.

The shell recognizes the following wildcards:

`*`	any character string, up to the maximum allowable length
`?`	exactly 1 character
`[abx]`	only one character, `a`, `b` or `x`
`[1-9]`	any one character, from 1 to 9

In some preceding examples the * wildcard was already used.

Examples:

`rm a*`	remove a, a1, axyz, ...
`rm a*b`	remove ab, acb, axyzb, ...
`rm ?`	remove a, b, c, ...
`rm a??b`	remove aaab, aabb, aacb, ...
`rm dat[ei]x`	remove datex and datix
`rm dat[e-g]x`	remove datex, datfx and datgx
`rm dat[efg]x`	same effect as the last example

Note that special characters recognized by the shell can be canceled with the backslash (\\) character.

`rm  \?*`	removes ?, ?a, ?abc, ...

The examples presented above can be dangerous. It would be less risky to use: `rm -i` for interactive removal.

Of course wildcards are valid with other commands as well. For example: `chmod 700 *` changes the access rights to all files in the current directory.

Exercises:

1.) Copy the `/etc/passwd` file under the name "`user`" in the login directory.

2.) Determine what access rights exist for the three user classes for the file user.

3.) Which of the following files are removed by the following commands?

a)	`rm`	`?`	Files:	`a, b, cd, e`
b)	`rm`	`x??y`	Files:	`xaby, xabcy`
c)	`rm`	`\?*`	Files:	`?, ?xzb, a?bc`
d)	`rm`	`a[a-z]1`	Files:	`aa1, a1b, az1`

4.) All C source programs in the directory `/usr/u2/cprog` should be displayed on the screen and removed. How is the command written? Remember that all C source programs normally have the "`.c`" extension in their filenames.

8. Filters and Pipes

8.1   Input/Output Redirection: Filter

A filter is a program with the following characteristics:

1.)   It reads from the standard input (`stdin`).

2.)   It writes to the standard output (`stdout`).

3.)   Error messages go to the standard error output (`stderr`).

Many commands are filters. Also, user programs should be written as a filter whenever possible. Filters follow a virtual file concept. The following are pre-set:

Filter	Medium
stdin	Keyboard
stdout	Display
stderr	Display

Through redirection on the shell level (the programs remain undisturbed) other files can be attached via redirection.

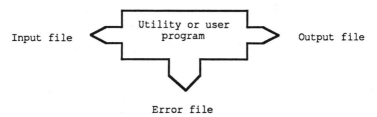

Input file   Utility or user program   Output file

Error file

Figure 19.1

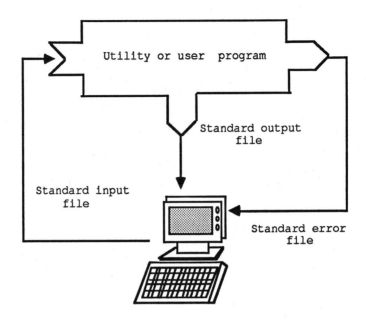

Figure 19.2

The following redirection characters can be used:

>   Output redirection: old file content, if present, is overwritten.

>>:   Output redirection: output is appended to the old file content, if present.

2>   Output redirection for stderr.

1>&2>   Standard channel 1 is redirected to channel 2.

<   Input redirection.

The effect of the redirection character will be explained on the basis of a few examples.

Output redirection:

Input: `ls / >content` or: `cat   content`

Outputs: `bin`
                `dev`
                `etc`
                `lib`
                `tmp`
                `unix`
                `usr`   ...and probably many other files

Input: `ls >/dev/tty08`

Outputs the list on display terminal 8, if the screen is active and the user did not set `mesg n`.

Input: `who >>content`

Adds the list of active users to the file content.

Input Redirection:

Input: `wc <content`

Counts the number of lines, words and characters in the file content.

Redirection of the Error Message:

Input: `cat  nodat  2>ferr`

The error message will appear in the `ferr` file. Output from the `cat` command is still as normal. If the `nodat` file does not exist, the `cat` command will produce an error message.

Combinations of Redirection:

Input: `wc  <data_in  >data_out  2>ferr`

An error message results in file `ferr` only if the file `data_in` does not exist. Otherwise, the result of the command is in the file `data_out`.

8.2   Pipe Mechanism

Pipes are nameless "RAM files" which, from the viewpoint of the user, are transparent. Several filters can be connected into strings with the help of pipes. The `stdout` of the first filter becomes the `stdin` of the second filter, and so on.

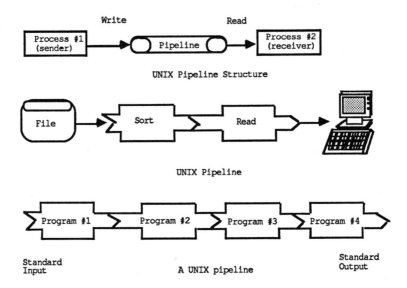

Figure 20

Temporary files for intermediate storage are not required. The pipe character is the vertical line (|). Powerful super commands can be generated with the help of pipes.

Some examples for simple pipe applications:

    who | wc -l   returns the number of active users

    ls /bin | more   creates paged display output

While input and output files can be redirected with the help of the > and < characters, the | character permits the direct connection of various programs without having to indicate intermediate storage files. To achieve the effect of:

    who | wc -l

with the input/output redirection, the following must be input:

```
who  >tempdat
wc  -l  <tempdat
```

This is obviously more complicated. Furthermore, an unnecessary auxiliary file is created. The input:

```
who  >wc  -l
```

will not work, because wc -l is a program (command) and not a file. Instead, an attempt is made to output to file wc which fails because of the write protection.

TEE

Syntax: tee [options] [file1] ...

Function: Creates a T piece between stdin and stdout. The output also goes to the additional files indicated.

Options: -i   Interrupts should be ignored.
              -a   Output should be appended to the existing file without overwrite existing data, same effect as in >>.

Example:

```
sort -u content | tee sort_content | lpr
```
              Content is sorted line by line and output on the display (stdout). The same data is also sent to the file sort_content and to the printer.

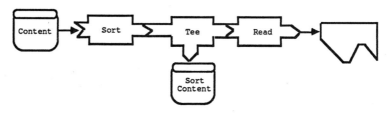

Figure 21

Exercises:

Use the `cat` command as a simple editor by redirecting the standard output:

1.) Write a line containing the word "`date`" into the info file.

   The `cat` command reads from `stdin` and then outputs the information read to `stdout`.

   As the last input line, `cat` requires <Crtl><D>.

2.) Append the following lines to the `info` file with the help of the `cat` command:

   ```
   echo  "Number of active users: \c"
   who  |  wc  -l
   ```

3.) Verify the content of the `info` file with the `cat` command.

4.) The `info` file created is actually a shell procedure. The shell itself can be called with: `sh filename`.

   If the filename is indicated, shell did not read from `stdin`, but from the file.

   Execute the first shell procedure.

5.) After every login, shell executes the commands in the `.profile` file if it is present. The `.profile` file must be in the user's home login directory.

   Enter the following lines into the `.profile` file:

   ```
   clear
   sh  info
   ```

   End the session and start a new session (login) to see the results when the `.profile` file created is executed.

Solutions:

1.) `cat  >info`
     `date`
     `<Crtl><D>`

2.) `cat  >>info`
     `echo  "Number of current users: \c"`
     `who  |  wc  -l`
     `<Crtl><D>`

3.) `cat  info`

4.) `sh  info`

5.) `cat  >.profile`
     `clear`
     `sh  info`
     `<Crtl><D>`

9. Frequently Used Commands

Some of the more frequently used commands are presented here in alphabetical order. Several of these commands have beeen covered, but are presented here again in more detail.

The following commands are described:

cal	mail
cancel	mesg
cat	more
clear	page
comm	passwd
crypt	pr
date	ps
du	sort
echo	split
file	tail
grep	time
head	wc
login	who
lp	write
lpstat	

CAL

Syntax: cal [mm] yyyy

Function: Creates calendar excerpts.

Options: None

MS-DOS: —

Examples:

cal 01 1987
> Displays a calender for the month of January 1987.

cal 1987
> Displays a calendar for all 12 months in 1987.

CANCEL

Syntax: `cancel [request-id ...] [printer...]`

Function: Print requests made with `lp` or `lpr` are canceled.

Options: None

MS-DOS: —

Remark: `Request-id` is the designation used in the `lp` or `lpr` command. If the printer is indicated, the currently active printer is interrupted (see also `lpstat`).

Examples:

`cancel test`
The print assignment with the `request-id` test is canceled.

CAT

Syntax: `cat [options] [file1] ...`

Function: Writes the files indicated to `stdout`.

Options: Specified by the manufacturer. Check the UNIX manuals for the operating system in use.

MS-DOS: `type file`

Examples:

    `cat`

Reads from `stdin`, writes to `stdout`.

    `cat   text1`
The file `text1` is output to `stdout`.

    `cat   >screenin`
Reads from `stdin` (keyboard) to EOF and writes everything into the file `screenin`.

    `cat   a   b   c   >d`
Sequentially copies the files `a`, `b` and `c` into file `d` (chaining function).

CLEAR

Syntax:	`clear`
Function:	Clears the display screen.
Options:	None
Remark:	Not available on all systems.
MS-DOS:	`cls`
Example:	`clear` The user's display screen is cleared.

COMM

Syntax: `comm [options] dat1 dat2`

Function: Displays the lines common to files `dat1` and `dat2` (Note that the files must be sorted).

Three columns are output:
    Column 1: Lines which occur only in `dat1`
    Column 2: Lines which occur only in `dat2`
    Column 3: Lines which occur in both

Options: `-1`
              `-2`   (see below)
              `-3`
              `-`   Input from `stdin`

Options `1,2` and `3` suppress output of the corresponding columns or lines in the default output. They can be combined however you like. If a number is omitted, then the input is taken from the `stdin`.

MS-DOS: —

Example:

    `comm  -3  a  b`
    All lines which occur exclusively in file a are output in the first column. All lines which are only available in file b appear in the second column.

    `comm  -12  a  b`
    All lines which appear in both files are output.

    `comm  -23  a  b`
    All lines which occur only in file a are output.

CRYPT

Syntax: `crypt [key]`

Function: Encodes and decodes text. The text becomes unreadable to users who do not know the key.

Remark: `Crypt` is a filter (reads from `stdin`, writes to `stdout`). To encode the file content, use the redirection mechanism of the shell. This command is generally only available within the United States.

Caution: The key can be any character string. A user who forgets the key loses the contents of the file. Even the super-user cannot help recover the file contents if the key is lost. Also, encrypted files should not be concatenated or you may not be able to recover the data.

MS-DOS: —

Examples:

`crypt  aaaa  <clear_dat  >secret_dat`
Reads standard text from the file `clear_dat`, encodes it with the `aaaa` key, and writes the encoded text into the file `secret_dat`.

`crypt  aaaa  <secret_dat`
Reads the encoded text from the file `secret_dat` using the key of `aaaa`, and outputs the clear text to `stdout` (display screen).

`crypt  <secret_dat`
If a key is not indicated in the `crypt` command, a prompt appears requesting the desired key. Input at this time is not echoed to the screen.

DATE

Syntax: `date [date, time]`

Function: Outputs the date and time when no parameters are specified. Only the super-user is allowed to modify or set the system date and time.

Remark: The format and type of date expected by the `date` command is machine dependent. Check the UNIX manuals for the system you are using for the proper syntax.

MS-DOS: `date`
                `time`

Example:

`date`   Returns date and time.

`date 8701231415`
                Sets date to 23 January, 1987 and time to 14:15 (super-user).

`date "+Date:%d.%m.%yn   Time:%M:%H"`
                Returns the following output (SysteV):
                `Date: 14.01.88, Time: 10:55.`

D U

Syntax: `du [option] [dat1] ...`

Function: Returns the disk usage or block assignment of the files indicated.

Options: `-a`   Block number for each file (default).
              `-s`   Only the total number of blocks is indicated.

MS-DOS: —

Example:

    `du   /work/program/books`
      Outputs the block assignment of the specified files.

    `du   -s  /usr/u30`
      Outputs the total block assignment of the indicated directory including all of its files.

ECHO

Syntax: echo [arguments] [\character]

Function: Output of commentary in shell procedures.

Options: System dependent.

Examples:

    echo   "Good Day \c"
    Outputs the comment "Good Day" on stdout, with
    no line feed. Various C language escape conventions
    using the backslash character (such as the \c to
    suppress the line feed) may be supported, check the
    system documentation for the system being used.

    echo   /usr/u?
    Returns a list of all applicable file names of the form:
    /usr/u1, ...u2, ...u3, ...

MS-DOS: rem

Remark: When possible, the arguments are evaluated as in the
                 second example presented above. More about this in
                 Chapters 12 and 13.

FILE

Syntax: `file [options] file1 ...`

Function: Attempts to determine the type of the specified files
                (many classes exist, such as C program text, object
                files, etc.). This command uses information in the
                `/etc/magic` file to help identify certain system
                specific files.

Options: Machine dependent

MS-DOS: —   File types are identified by the use of standard
                         filename extensions.

Example:

`file /usr/u4/*`
                All files of the indicated directory are checked. Output
                of the results is sent to `stdout`.

GREP

Syntax:	`grep [options] expression [file1] ...`
Function:	Searches the specified files for text patterns which were indicated in expression. The matching line is output. Metacharacters such as the asterisk, question mark, etc. are permitted if they are masked within quotes (".....).").

Options:

`-b`	Include block numbers.
`-c`	Count number of matching lines.
`-f file`	Search expression is in the indicated file and not in the argument.
`-h`	No filename in the output line.
`-n`	Output line numbers in every hit line.

`-s`	No output, only status for procedures:
	    0 = hit
	    1 = not hit
	    2 = syntax error

`-v`	Inversion of the command: The lines without hits are output.
`-y`	No distinction made between upper and lower case letters.

Other options exist.

MS-DOS:	—
Remark:	`egrep` and `fgrep` are modifications of the `grep` command.

Examples:

```
grep  -c  "Oma"  textfile
```
Counts and outputs the number of times the string
"Oma" occurs in the file textfile.

```
grep  -n  "A*"  /division/handball/members
```
All lines starting with "A", from the members file, are
output with their line number included.

HEAD

Syntax:	`head [option] [file1] ...`
Function:	The first n lines of `stdin`, or the `files` indicated, are output to `stdout`.
Options:	`-n` Indicates the number of lines from the beginning of the file to be included.
MS-DOS:	—
Example:	

```
head  -10  /usr/u3/cprog/*.c
```
The first 10 lines of all files in the indicated directory
with a `.c` suffix are output to `stdout`.

LOGIN

Syntax: `login [name]`

Function: Logs new users on the system and removes old users.

Options: None

MS-DOS: —

Example:

    `login u2`   Logs on user u2

Remark: Execution of the login procedure:

    1.   System asks for password.
    2.   Evaluates `/etc/passwd` and the user is assigned their login directory as the working directory.
    3.   Super-user messages from `/etc/motd` are output on `stdout`.
    4.   Message flags any mail which has arrived.
    5.   Execution of `/etc/profile`.
    6.   Execution of `.profile` (if standard shell).

Note that the logon sequence may not be the same for all systems.

LP

Syntax:	`lp [options] [file1] ...`
Function:	Inserts a print request into the wait queue of the Spool System. Requests are processed sequentially.

Options:

    -c   Creates a temporary `Copy` file. The original file remains accessible (for example for the editor).

    -m   After print output, a message is sent by mail to the originator.

    -r   Remove file after insertion of a temporary copy into the waiting queue.

Remark: May be replaced with the `lpr` command on some UNIX systems.

MS-DOS: `print file`

Example:

    `lp -cm text1`
    The file `text1` can still be processed further. After printout, a message is generated via mail to the user.

LPSTAT

Syntax: `lpstat [options] [request...]`

Function: Provides information for the spool system, including the current status of the print queue.

Options:

`-u [list]`
> Outputs the status of all print requests for users in the list specified, each separated by a comma.

Many other options are available.

MS-DOS: —

Example:

`lpstat  -u  u2,u3`
> Outputs the list of all print requests for users u2 and u3.

MORE and PG

Syntax:	`more [options] [file1] ...` `pg   [options] [file1] ...`
Function:	Display ready preparation of output with user controls for ease of viewing.
Options:	Many, see example.
Remark:	Mostly used as a filter to provide a manageable screen display. The `pg` command additionally may clear the screen.
MS-DOS:	`more`

Example:

`ls  -l | more`
Returns a display ready list. The display pauses when the screen is filled. Continue to the next screen by pressing the space key, or press <CR> for the next line. On most systems, pressing h will yield a list of available commands recognized by `more`.

PASSWD

Syntax:	`passwd [user-name]`
Function:	Change or define a (new) password.
Options:	None
MS-DOS:	---
Remark:	When changing an existing password, the system requests the old password first. The new password must then be input twice. The password should be at least 6 characters long. System V requests 6 characters with at least one number. The super-user can change or remove a password without knowing the old password. They can also use a shorter password, or one without numbers.

PR

Syntax:	`pr [options] [file1] ...`
Function:	Prepares files for printing.

Options:

-h   Following text is output as page header.

-l[n] n
Lines per page (standard is usually 66).

-n   n column output

n[nz] Line numbering:
n = Number size (standard = 5 digits)
z = Dividing character between line
numbers and line content
(a space is standard)

-o[n] n character spaces at the left border

-p[n] After n pages, wait so that paper can be changed (single page printer).

-t   Suppresses title, line numbers and date.

-w[n] Page width in characters.

Additional options exist.

MS-DOS: —

Remark: Generally used as a filter before the `lp` or `lpr` command, and is extremely useful.

Example:

```
pr -h "Headline" -172 dat1 | lp
```
Output (printer) the `dat1` file with header "Headline" and 72 lines per page.

```
pr -n /usr/u3/cprog/prog1.c | lp
```
Output a C source program `prog1.c` with 5 column line numbering.

P S

Syntax: `ps [options] [process1 ...] [user1 ...]`

Function: Gives status information about active processes.

The most important are:
the process number (`PID`)
the interactive terminal (`TTY`)
the computer time used (`TIME`)
the command call (`CMD`)

Options: `-a`   All interactive processes.

`-e`   All processes for all users.

`-f`   Complete information list.

`-l`   Long form of the information list.

`-u user`
All processes for the indicated users.

Additional system dependent options may exist.

MS-DOS: —

Example:

`ps -al` All interactive processes of the active user in the system are output in long form.

`ps -u u3`
All processes for user u3 are output.

`ps -e`   All processes for all users are output.

`ps 1036`
Only the process with `PID` `1036` is included.

SORT

Syntax: `sort [options] [+pos1] [-pos2] [file1] ...`

Function: Sorts the lines of all files indicated according to the ASCII character set (see Appendix). The parameters `+pos1` and `-pos2` restrict a sort key to one beginning at character position `pos1` and ending just before `pos2`.

Options: `-b`   Ignore blanks and tab characters at the beginning of the field.

              `-d`   Consider only alphanumeric characters and blanks (no special characters).

              `-f`   Treat uppercase letters as lowercase.

              `-n`   Sort numeric characters at the beginning of the field according to their numeric values.

              `-r`   Sort in reverse order.

              `-t [c]`   Dividing character c, may not be a space.

              Many other options exist.

MS-DOS: `sort < file1 > file2`

Remark: For a complete explanation of the syntax and other options, see the documentation for your specific UNIX system.

Examples:

```
sort   a  b  >ab
```
The files a and b are sorted, and stored in ab.

```
who | sort  -r
```
Returns a sorted list of users in reverse alphabetical order.

```
sort  -t:  +1
```
The data is sorted after the first column behind the colon ":" separator.

```
sort  +0  -1  +2  -3  +1n  -2
```
The data is sorted as follows:

1. according to the first field (+0 -1)
2. according to the third field (+2 -3)
3. according to the second field, numerically (+1n -2)

```
sort  +1,2  -2
```
The data is sorted according to the second field, starting at the third character (+1,2 -2).

SPLIT

Syntax:	`split [-n] [file [name]]`
Function:	Splits the indicated file into parts of n lines each. The output files are called `nameaa`, `nameab`, `nameac`, etc. The default for `name` is x.
Options:	`-n` Number of lines for each partial file. The default is 1,000 lines per file.
MS-DOS:	—
Example:	

```
split -66 text textline
```
The file is split and copied into smaller files
`textlineaa`, `textlineab`, `textlineac`, ... of
66 lines each.

TAIL

Syntax:	`tail [n [units]] [file1 ...]`
Function:	Copies the named file to `stdout`, beginning at a designated position within the file.
Options:	none
MS-DOS:	—
Remark:	n is the number in units from which printing should start:

+n   relative to start of file
-n   relative to end of file

Units are: c = characters
              l = lines (standard)
              b = blocks of 512 bytes each

Example:

```
tail  -100  texta  >textb
```
Copies the last 100 lines of the file texta into the file textb.

TIME

Syntax:	`time [command]`
Function:	Returns the execution time of a command or program with actual (real) delays, user mode (user), and system mode (sys) in seconds.
Options:	none
MS-DOS:	—
Remark:	Time precedes the command or program to be timed.
Example:	

    `time   who`

        Returns the execution time for the `who` command.

wc

Syntax:	`wc [options] [file1] ...`
Function:	Counts lines, words and/or characters in the indicated files.

Options: `-l`   count only lines
            `-w`   count only words
            `-c`   count only characters

MS-DOS: —

Example:

```
wc  text
```
Counts lines, characters and words in the file `text`.

```
who | wc  -l
```
Returns the number of current users by counting the number of lines which are output by the `who` command.

WHO

Syntax:	`who [am I]`
Function:	Returns information about current users, user identifications, terminals, start of session, etc.
Options:	See the documentation for your specific system.
MS-DOS:	—
Example:	

`who`   Information for all current users.

`who am I`
       Only the user's terminal.

10. Background Processing

Multi-processing:

The termination of a command line with the Return or Enter key <CR> causes the shell to begin execution of a process and wait for its completion. During this processing time, no other commands are accepted by the shell. However, a command can be executed in the "background", allowing other tasks to be accomplished. This is called *multi-processing*.

Background processing:

Background processing always makes sense if a command, or application program, can be executed as a batch job. This means that no interaction (no dialog) is required between the program and the user. Most of the usual UNIX commands are this type of program, for example:

```
who
wc
cp
cd
pwd
```

Executing these commands in the background is not efficient because their run-time is so short that little time is saved. Pure dialog commands, such as passwd, are not suitable for background processing.

What commands or programs should be considered? Those which generate little or no output to the screen, and take a relatively long time to execute.

Of the commands discussed up to now, this mainly includes the printer commands and the find command. While a command executes in the background, work can continue as a dialog with the shell. Precautions must be taken to prevent the intrusion of a message from the background command into the interactive dialog.

This can be particularly unpleasant during a session with an editor or a word processing program. The simplest way to prevent this is to redirect output of the background program to a file. Background processing is started with the ampersand "&" character. The general syntax is:

```
Command [options] [arguments]&
```

PID:

What happens after the start of the background processing? The shell issues the process ID number (PID) and is prepared to receive additional commands for other background processing. The termination of a process is not reported (unless generated by the process itself).

Information about any process can be obtained with the ps command. It returns the PID, plus other useful information about the process. If a process needs to be terminated prematurely, find the PID with the ps command and input the following:

```
kill  -9  pid
```

The kill command will not be discussed in great detail here. However, the general syntax is:

```
kill [-signal] pid
```

The signal "9" used above causes a sure termination of any process. Also, several processes can be terminated at the same time. For example:

```
kill  -9  1024  1036  946
```

would terminate all three processes listed. Entering a process ID (PID) of zero will terminate all active tasks. Of course the user can only terminate his own processes, except for the super-user who can kill any or all processes of any user.

The capability of terminating processes is another advantage of the background processing, because the shell remains available for input of additional commands, such as the kill command in this instance.

Two examples of background processing:

```
pr  -h  "Example 1"  prdat | lp&
            The prdat file is output to the printer with the
            heading "Example 1".
```

```
find  .  -name  "c*"  -print  >finddat&
```
A search is made, starting in the current working directory, for all files whose name starts with "c", with matching filenames listed in the finddat file.

Both of these examples require some time for execution and for this reason can be run in the background.

Exercises:

1.)   Start a print request and let it run in the background.

2.)   Execute other additional commands.

3.)   What process numbers were assigned?

4.)   Kill the print request.

11. Editors

At least two text editors, ed and sed, are generally available on every UNIX system. On many systems, the vi editor is also included. All three are rather old and do not contain many features found in newer text editors. However, the non-dialog oriented sed has a special use which justifies its existence.

Since several large programs are presented in the following chapters, the editors are only explained briefly enough to allow you to begin to use them in place of the cat command for creating files. The sed editor, which has significance in the "advanced" shell programming environment, is mentioned only briefly. The complicated vi editor is explained in a little more detail than ed, mainly because of its full screen orientation in contrast to the two other line oriented editors. If no other full screen editor is available, the use of vi during software generation is highly recommended. If a menu-controlled, full screen editor is available it will make your work much easier.

UNIX editors:

ed:
- line oriented
- interactive
- relatively easy to learn

sed:
- line oriented
- not interactive
- for batch processing

vi:
- most powerful UNIX editor
- interactive
- full screen capability
- unusual commands

Editors which are system dependent:
- not portable
- full screen capability
- interactive
- menu controlled
- fairly simple usage

11.1 ed

ed is a line oriented editor which remains from the days when teletypewriters (TTYs) were used as interactive terminals. On the basis of its line oriented characteristics, ed can be used in shell procedures. However, since ed is interactive it can also be used for text input as well.

The maximum line length of an ed file is typically 512 characters. That is more than most modern editors normally tolerate, which is typically around 128 or 256 characters per line.

The general call for ed is:

```
ed [-] [-x] [file]
```

If a file was indicated, the file content is read into a temporary buffer for processing. Otherwise, the keyboard (stdin) serves as the only input medium.

The file content is written back with:

```
w [file]
```

If the content of the file is written back to the same file, the filename does not have to be indicated.

When opening and closing files, ed indicates how many characters were read from, or written to, the disk file. This can be suppressed with the "-" option.

ed is terminated with the letter "q", short for quit. If the buffer was changed without writing it back, ed reports a question mark "?" to warn that the file was not saved. A new input of q at this warning terminates the session without saving the buffer contents.

When the -x option is used with the ed command, a password is required as the next input in order to access the file. This is used for encryption and decoding of the text in the file.

Text input using ed

Here is a list of commands which initiate input mode within ed (items in brackets are optional):

`[line]a`	(append)	Add text after the current [indicated] line.
`[line]i`	(insert)	Insert text before the current [indicated] line.
`[area]c`	(change)	Replace the current line [of the indicated area] with the following text.
`.`		Terminate the input mode.

Line and area indications:

`.`	Current line
`$`	Last line
`n`	Specific line number n
`+n`	Line n lines after the current line
`-m`	Line m lines before the current line
`n,m`	Range of lines, from line n to line m
`/pattern/`	Next line containing the pattern
`?pattern?`	Preceding line containing the pattern

Examples for line and area indications:

`28`	Line 28
`4,8`	Range of lines, from lines 4 to 8
`1,$`	The entire buffer
`.-2,.+9`	Two lines before the current line to 9 lines after the current line (periods cannot be omitted).
`/Peter/,/Karl/`	Area from the line containing the pattern "Peter" up to the line with the pattern "Karl" (search forward starting from the current line).

115

Exercise

Remember to terminate each line with <CR>:

Input	Comment
ed	Call of ed
a	Start input mode (append)
Hello Peter	Input line 1
Peter, hello	Input line 2
.	Text end, terminate input mode
w ed_file	Store in ed_file
q	Terminate ed
ed ed_file	New call to ed with the same file
2a	Input after line 2
This is Line 3	Input new line 3
1	Line pointer to line 1
i	Enter Insert mode
The new Line 1	New input new line 1
.	Text end, terminate input mode
w	Store in ed_file again
q	Terminates ed

The user should also be able to erase areas of lines, replace lines, change lines or display them on the screen.

Additional ed commands (items in [] are optional):

`[area]d`	(delete)	Deletes the current line [the indicated area].
`e file`	(edit)	Reads the file into the working buffer. The old contents are erased.
`f`	(filename)	Outputs the name of the processed files.
`g/pattern/ed`	(global)	Performs the command for all lines containing the pattern.
`v/pattern/ed`	(inVert)	Performs the command for all lines which do not contain the pattern.
`[area]j`	(join)	Combine the lines [of the indicated area] into one line.
`[area]l`	(list)	Outputs the current line [the indicated area]. Non-printing characters are displayed.
`[area]p`	(print)	Outputs the current line [the indicated area].
`[line]r file`	(read)	Reads and inserts the specified file behind the current [indicated] line in the working buffer.
`/pattern/`	(search)	Searches for the next line, after the current line, which contains the pattern. This line then becomes the current line.

`[area]s/pattern/new_text/[g][n]`

(substitute) Replaces the pattern in the current line with `new_text`. If g is indicated, every occurrence is replaced; otherwise only the first occurrence in each line. If a number n appears after the command, only the nth occurrence of the matched string on each line is replaced.

`[area]m[line]`	(move)	Copies the text of the current line [of the indicated area] after the current [or indicated] line. If [line] is specified, the original is erased.
`[area]t[line]`	(transfer)	As in move, but the original line remains unchanged.
`u`	(undo)	Reverses the last change in the buffer.
`! command`		Executes the shell command.

`ed` also recognizes various characters with special significance (metacharacters). For example, enclosing brackets "`[....]`" and the asterisks "`*`" are permitted in a search pattern. The effects are the same as on the shell level (see Wildcards in Chapter 7). The double-slash "`//`" metacharacter, entered by itself, causes renewed forward searching.

The last exercise can be continued with:

Input	Comment
`ed ed_file`	Call of `ed` to edit previous file
`g/Peter/`	Prints the lines containing "`Peter`"
`1d`	Erases line 1
`1`	Line pointer to 1
`1,$ s/Peter/Karl/g`	Replace all occurrences of "`Peter`" with "`Karl`"
`1,$ p`	Print the entire file
`w`	Store in `ed_file`
`q`	Terminates `ed`

Keep in mind that `ed` only operates in one of two modes: the *command mode* and the *input mode*.

With commands such as: `d, p or !`
        `ed` remains in the command mode.

With the commands: `a, i and c`
        `ed` enters the input mode.

When a period (`.`) is entered alone at the beginning of an input line, `ed` leaves input mode and returns to command mode.

Exercises:

What are the appropriate ed commands to accomplish the following?

1.)   Find the words "Unix" or "unix".

2.)   Add text to the beginning, or end, of the buffer.

3.)   Output lines 1 to 5.

4.)   Output the last 3 lines of the buffer.

5.)   Erase from the current line to the pattern "UNIX".

6.)   Find the next occurrence of a two digit number.

7.)   Perform the same search again.

8.)   Replace every repeated occurrence of the "#" character, in all
       lines, with a single "#" character.

9.)   Replace every repeated occurrence of the "*" character in a line,
       with a single "*" character.

10.)   Replace "a*b" with "a&b".

11.)   Erase all lines that start with a plus-sign "+".

12.)   Replace "X" with "X\n".

Solutions:

1.)   `g/[Uu]nix/l//`

2.)   To enter text at the beginning of the file:

1	(or 0a)	Position to start of file
i		Enter input (insert) mode, to add text before the first line
text_line_1		
text_line_2		Enter desired text
text_line_n		
.		Terminate input mode

To enter text at the end of the file:

$	(or $a)	Position to end of file
a		Enter input (append) mode, to add text after the last line
text_line_1		
text_line_2		Enter desired text
text_line_3		
.		Terminate input mode

3.)   `1,5  p`   Or use: `1,5  l`

4.)   `$-2,  $p`

5.)   `.g/UNIX/d`

6.)   `g/[0-9][0-9]/l`

7.)   `//`

8.)   `1,$s/## */#/g`

9.)   `s/\*\**/\*/g`

10.)   `.$s/a\*b/a\&b/l`

11.)   `1,$v/+/d`

12.)   `1,$/X/X\\n/g`

11.2 sed

While `ed` is an interactive editor, `sed` can be considered the non-interactive version of `ed` from the standpoint of functionality and user interface. The design of `sed` differs basically from `ed`.

The `sed` editor is constructed in such a manner as to be suitable for the following applications:

- Editing of files which are too large for an interactive editor, such as `vi`.

- Editing of files if:

    * The commands are too complicated for interactive input.

    * The number of commands to be input interactively is too large.

If no input files are indicated, `sed` reads from the standard input (`stdin`).

The general call for `sed` is:

```
sed [-n] [-e script] [-f cmd_file] [input_file ...]
```

The content of the `input_file` is copied to `stdout`, with the relevant lines edited per the specified commands.

Options:　　`-e`　　`sed` commands can be indicated directly (beware of the shell metacharacters!).

　　　　　　`-f`　　`sed` commands are read from the specified command file, with one command per line.

　　　　　　`-n`　　suppresses the standard output.

This brief amount of information is sufficient for an introduction to `sed` and is not meant to be a complete tutorial.

11.3 vi

In contrast to ed and sed, vi is oriented toward the display screen.

Advantages:

- ed can be called within vi.

- Numerous commands.

- Can work with intelligent and fast terminals, as well as devices with slow transmission rates.

- Undo function.

- Places small load on the UNIX system processor.

Disadvantages:

- Difficult to learn.

- Unusual user interface.

- Missing feedback: user does not see where he works (input mode or command mode). Plus, no feedback during "dangerous" inputs.

Introduction:

vi was developed by Bill Joy of the Electrical Engineering and Computer Science Department at the University of California, Berkeley Campus. It provides a full screen, interactive text editor for working on files. The editor does not work directly with the files, but uses a copy of the file in a working buffer. This makes it possible to undo serious errors or erroneous commands or even abort an entire editing session.

Since there are numerous commands in vi, and many are difficult to learn, only a small number of the actual commands will be discussed. This abbreviated command set should be sufficient to create and store a file.

Creating a file

To create a file, simply input the program name vi, followed by the desired filename:

```
vi  filename  <CR>
```

This command creates the indicated file, clears the display screen, and positions the cursor at the upper left corner of the screen.

Text input

To input text, vi must be first placed in the text insert mode. This is done by entering one of the following commands:

a	(append)	append text
i	(insert)	insert text
o	(open)	insert new line (implies i)

Note that no return <CR> is used with these commands, they are executed immediatly after pressing the single key indicated.

After one of these commands has been input, the text can then be entered normally, as in any other text editor.

Terminating the text insert mode

To leave the text insert mode, press the Escape <Esc> key. The cursor is moved back one column, and vi is switched back to the command mode.

Writing back the file

Since the text is stored only in an internal buffer of vi, it must be written to a permanent storage device. If this is omitted, the text is lost when you exit vi. To write the text into a disk file, use the write command, or its abbreviated form w preceded by a colon:

```
:write <CR>        or      :w  <CR>
```

The colon (:) is essential. The colon switches vi into the command line mode, where commands can be entered on the lower left corner of the display. Note that commands entered here must be terminated with the return <CR>.

vi then copies its internal buffer to the indicated file. If the file does not yet exist, vi will display a message containing the filename followed by "NEW FILE" and the number of characters written. The buffer still remains available and unchanged for additional editing.

It is a good idea to use the w command periodically to prevent the loss of the complete text during a systems crash.

If vi was called without a filename, it cannot create a new file. This can be remedied by the input of:

```
:w   filename   <CR>
```

The buffer is then written to the named file and you can precede as normal.

Leaving the editor

When finished editing the file, there are several methods of leaving the vi editor and returning to the shell:

- If the text was already written back to the file, simply input this command to quit:

    ```
    :q   <CR>
    ```

- To write the text back to the file and leave the vi editor at the same time, input any of the following commands:

    ```
    :wx   <CR>
    :x    <CR>
    <shift> ZZ   (without <CR>)
    ```

- To leave vi without writing the text back to the file, use the following command:

    ```
    :q!   <CR>
    ```

    The exclamation mark following the "q" forces vi to leave the program without changing the original text file.

Editing an existing file

To edit an existing file, input:

```
vi filename <CR>
```

The indicated file is read directly into the internal buffer of vi, and is available on the screen for changes.

If the editor issues a "NEW FILE" message, an input error probably occurred in typing. Leave the editor with :q or :q! and try again.

Readonly mode

The vi editor has a readonly mode that is entered by using the view command instead of vi:

```
view filename <CR>
```

With this command, a normal entry is made to the editor. If a write command is entered, the following message appears:

```
"filename" File is readonly
```

To force the overwrite of the file, you can input the write command with an exclaimation mark:

```
:w! <CR>
```

Moving the cursor through a file

vi has many commands for moving through a file. Travel can be page by page, forward or backward. There is also direct access to lines through the indication of a line number or a search string.

A simple example for this would be:

```
:5   <CR>
```

This command positions the cursor to the beginning of line 5 in the file.

Paging through the text

In vi there are 2 ways of paging through the text.

1.)   Scrolling

2.)   Paging by page

Scrolling

The Scroll command permits paging through the file on the display without having to construct or clear the screen. The commands are as follows:

           `<Ctrl><D>`   = Page down

           `<Ctrl><U>`   = Page up

Note that some terminals do not support paging up. These terminals first clear the screen and then build a new display.

To view a few lines above or below the current display, the commands for line scrolling can be used:

           `<Ctrl><E>`   = One line down

           `<Ctrl><Y>`   = One line up

Paging by page

Paging by page moves through the file by clearing the screen with every command and displaying the next complete page of the text. The paging commands are as follows:

           `<Ctrl><F>`   = Page forward one page

           `<Ctrl><B>`   = Page backward one page

Moving the cursor within the line

The following commands move the cursor a character or word at a time within the line. If the command is preceded by a number, the command is repeated that many times.

b	beginning of the preceding word
e	end of the next word
h	cursor one position left
l	cursor one position right
w	beginning of the next word
B	beginning of previous word, without stopping at periods.
W	beginning of the next word, without stopping at periods
`<BS>`	cursor one position left (Backspace)
`<SP>`	cursor one position right (Space)

Note that on some terminals various cursor keys can be used for cursor movement, but this is not standard.

Change the line

There are many commands to change the line. Each of these commands (with the exception of commands H, L and M) can be preceded by a number to repeat the command.

j	Cursor one line down
k	Cursor one line up
<Return>	
	Cursor to the first position of the next line
+	Cursor to the first word of the next line
−	Cursor to the first word of the previous line
H	Cursor to the first line of the display
M	Cursor to the middle of the display
L	Cursor to the last line of the display

Searching with vi

Another form of text positioning results from letting the editor search for a pattern and then displaying the text found. To search for text, use slash before and after the desired search-pattern in the command:

```
/search-pattern/ <CR>
```

Starting at the current cursor position, a search is made for the search-pattern and the cursor is positioned to the location where it is found. If the search-pattern was not found, the following message:

```
Pattern not found
```

is displayed on the last line of the display. To search backward through the text, use question marks before and after the search-pattern:

```
?search-pattern? <CR>
```

If the pattern was not found by the end of the file, the search is normally continued at the beginning of the file. The search continues to the position in the file where the search command was originally started. To search only to the end of the file, an internal option of vi can be set with the following command:

```
:set nowrapscan <CR>        or      :set nows <CR>
```

To prevent discrimination by the editor between upper and lowercase letters, input the command:

    :set ignorecase <CR>   or   :set ic <CR>

The command:

    :set noic <CR>

switches vi back into the normal mode again for case recognition.

Repeated searches

If the text found by vi is not the desired occurrence, the search can be continued with the n command. The n command functions for the forward and backward searches. If the search-pattern should be changed between backward and forward searches, use:

    / <CR>

for forward searches, or:

    ? <CR>

for backward searches.

Special search characters

The vi editor recognizes some characters which have special significance within a search-pattern. These characters can be used when the word to be found is not precisely known. For example, it may only be known that the word starts with "A" and ends with "Z". These special characters act as spacers inside the search-pattern.

The special characters recognized by vi include:

(period)

> This special character stands for any character at the location where it appears in the search-pattern.

Example: Assume that a file has a line with the content `"vi editor"` or an expression with another character between `"vi edit"` and `"r"`. To find these lines, the following can be entered:

`/vi edit.r/  <CR>`

* (Asterisk)

This special character stands for any desired number of repeated characters. The character which is repeated precedes the asterisk `"*"`.

Example: Assume a file has the expression `"the xxxx editor"` and the user does not know how many x's appear in the search-pattern. The text can be found with the command:

`/the x* editor/  <CR>`

$ (Dollar Sign)

This special character is used within the search-pattern to indicate the end of the line.

Example: To search for all lines that end with the word "UNIX", enter:

`/UNIX$/  <CR>`

^ (circumflex)

This special character is the opposite of the dollar sign. It designates the beginning of the line.

Example: To search for all lines whose first character is an "A", input:

`/^A/  <CR>`

Masking the special character

As in the UNIX shell, the significance of the special characters can be masked by placing the backslash in front of the character.

Combining special characters

Special characters can be combined within a search-pattern.

Example: To search for all words on a single line starting
                with "A" and ending in "Z", input the following
                command:

        /^A.*Z$/   <CR>

The goto command

A specific line within the file can be accessed directly with the goto
command, even if that line is not on the current display screen. The
syntax used for this command is:

        <n>G

Where <n> is the line number to be found. To move directly to line
100, enter:

        100G

You should be able to find the line number of the current line by
pressing <Ctrl><G>.

Return to previous position

After a goto or search command was executed, entering two back
quotes (`) will return the cursor to its previous position. Keep in mind,
however, that this only works for the goto and search commands.
If you reposition the cursor after the goto or search command, the
back quotes will not return you to the original position in the file.

In summary

In some areas vi resembles ed, but they are in fact very different. To
really get the most use of vi, the material presented here should be
reinforced with several exercises, and possibly referring to additional
reference material. As you gain more experience with any of the UNIX
editors, many books are available that discuss the editors in great detail
for the more advanced user.

11.4 Other editors

The original UNIX editors were either line oriented (ed, sed) or keyboard independent (vi) because they used the Control key, instead of the function keys (which are not present on all terminals). The result is easy portability at the cost of user-friendliness. Since the various manufacturers' software must compete against each other in the market, its imperative for them to offer a modern, full-featured, and user-friendly editor.

An editor of this type should be display oriented with the basic functions selectable from a menu. The cursor keys and function keys (which are often programmable) of the standard terminals should be used. The files created with the help of one of these editors must not differ from any other UNIX file, and any of the original UNIX editors should be able to use these files.

The only disadvantage is that a special editor such as this, can usually run only on the products of one manufacturer. Since most users work primarily with only one type of system, this should not be a major disadvantage. The user should find the most user-friendly and easiest to use editor available for their particular system, even if it is dependent on the system manufacturer. After all, the editor is generally the most often used tool on the system.

12. The Shell as a Programming Language

The shell has many useful characteristics which have been previously described. The remainder of this chapter will cover additional shell functions and features. Those already discussed include:

- Interactive command interpretation

- Background processing (batch)

- Input/output redirection

- Pipelines

- Wildcard usage

The following three characteristics are described in this section:

Shell variables:

> The user can control the execution of the shell, plus other programs and utilities, through data stored in variables.

Shell procedures (scripts):

> A series of frequently used shell commands can be stored in a file. The name of the file can then be used later to execute this stored sequence with one simple command.

Programming language constructions:

> The shell has capabilities which permit its use as a programming language. These features can be used to create shell procedures to perform very complex operations.

> The purpose of procedures is to simplify usage of the operating system. The user can write "super commands" which can be defined to cover specific needs.

> An important special application is system control, such as automatic storage of files according to certain criteria, operation statistics and reports, etc.

12.1 Processes

To understand the characteristics and capabilities of the shell procedures, some theoretical considerations must be applied to the concept of the UNIX process. The process hierarchy is structured like a tree (dendritic) and resembles the file system. A parent process can produce offspring processes, which can then become the parent process of new offspring processes, and so on.

What is meant by "process"?

A process is the execution of a program, or more precisely an "image." An "image" includes everything a program requires to execute.

It contains:

- Image of the storage (with program code and data)

- Values in the registers

- Conditions of the open files

- Current file directory

- Program counter

- Status register

- Environment variables

During execution, the "image" must be in main memory.

After login, the shell is the only (user specific) active process (the login shell). This can be verified with the ps command. If, for example, the ls command is executed, the shell duplicates itself. The copy is overlaid on the ls program while the original shell waits for completion of the copy. The copy of a shell is called a "subshell."

The following diagram explains the example.

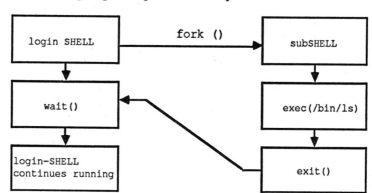

Figure 22

fork(), exec(), wait(), exit()

These are all "system calls", but represent only a very small portion of those available in UNIX. These four sytem calls regulate process generation and synchronization. They are used by the operating system itself, in addition to being available to users. For example, they can be started from within a C program. They have been implemented as commands which, among other things, are important within shell procedures.

The four system calls have the following effect:

fork()

Generates a copy of a process with the same image. The original is designated as the *parent process*, the copy is the *child process*. Both processes continue to run in the same environment, and with the same program counter. Parent and child processes are identified on the basis of the value which is returned by the fork call as status:

0   Child process

>0   Parent process (PID of the child)

−1   Child process could not be generated (too many child processes exist)

135

exec(file,argl,...)

Overlays the program and data segments of the current process with the program which is stored in the specified file, and executes it with the arguments indicated.

wait(status)

Causes the parent process to wait until a child process has finished. Wait returns the process number of the child (or an error code in the "status" variable).

exit(status)

Terminates a process and activates a parent process which may be waiting.

Example: exec ("who")

If a command is started as a background process, the wait call in the example is dropped (see Fig. 22).

Exercise:

Start a background process with a long execution time, such as a `find` command. Input the `ps` command in the foreground and observe the number of processes, as well as the process numbers (PIDs) of each processes.

Start the same background process several times in sequence. Verify the process hierarchy each time with the `ps` command.

12.2 Shell variables

Every programming language, including the shell, contains variables. There are various types of shell variables, as will be shown, but the data is always saved in a shell variable as a character string. Numerical variables do not exist, but shell variables can be used for calculations. More about this later.

Shell variables

The names of shell variables are freely definable, but can only consist of letters and numbers. The first character must be a letter or an underscore character. The assignment is made with the equal sign.

Enter the following at your terminal:

```
a=Ciao
b=Ciao Petra        (not permitted, 2 character strings!)
c="Ciao Petra"
d=51
```

If the shell variable is preceded by a dollar sign ($) character, the shell recognizes it is a variable and uses its current value.

Enter the following at your terminal:

```
echo  $a  $b  $c  $d
```

Shell variables are valid only within the shell in which they were created. The values of shell variables can only be used in a subshell if they were previously "exported" in the higher level shell. However, shell variables of a subshell cannot be read by a higher level shell.

Enter the following at your terminal:

```
export  a  b
sh
echo  $a  $b  $c  $d
<Ctrl><D>
```

With the `export` command, the variables a and b are exported and made available to the subshell created by the `sh` command. The `echo` command then displays the current shell variable contents from within the subshell. The <Ctrl><D> finally terminates the subshell.

`Export` is valid for all subshells.

If an exported shell variable in a subshell is changed (assigned another content), it must be exported again via the `export` command to make the changed variable known to subordinate subshells.

Shell variables are stored in central storage.

The shell variables are maintained in main memory, they are not stored on disk. After the shell variables are removed from the system, they're lost unless some background processes are still active which use the variables.

Pre-defined variables of the shell

Some shell variables have special significance for the shell. They have pre-defined values.

The names and current values of these *environment variables* can be output with the `set` command (without arguments). Pre-defined shell variables must be exported if their values are changed and they will be used in a subshell.

HOME   Name of the user's home directory. The shell uses this name when no directory name is indicated for the `cd` command.

PATH   A list of directories to be searched by the shell to find programs whose names are typed as commands. The `path` can include multiple entries separated by colons. The list is searched in the order given, left to right.

                        Standard: `PATH=.:/bin:/usr/bin`

PS1   The string to be used by the shell to prompt for the next command.

                        Standard: `"$"`   for users
                                           `"#"`   for super-user

MAIL   Pathname of the mail file for the UNIX mail facility.

LOGNAME   The user's login name (System V).

Note that capitalization is significant and there are many other pre-defined shell variables.

Some Explanations:

HOME   This variable can be used to change the working directory through the input of the cd command (without argument). The home directory then becomes the working directory.

Example:

```
HOME=/usr/u3/cprog
cd
pwd    --> returns
/usr/u3/cprog
```

PATH   MS-DOS also uses PATH. Not as a variable, but as a command. The PATH variable permits the start of programs without giving the full pathname, even if the program is in a directory other than the working directory. The corresponding directory (complete pathname) must be assigned to the shell variable PATH.

A permanent assignment of the shell variables can be achieved with the .profile file. This is interesting in connection with the pre-defined shell variables. However, remember that the variables defined in .profile must be exported to make them valid in the login shell and its subshells!

Quoting

With the use of metacharacters, the shell is informed which replacements should be made before the execution of a command. The following characters have special meaning to the shell unless quoted:

```
? * [...] <> $ | >>
```

In connection with the shell variables, the replacement mechanism is controlled by several special characters:

'string'   Apostrophe (single quote): No replacements should be made in the string.

Input: echo $HOME '$HOME'

"string"   Quotation marks: Only shell variables should be
             replaced in the string. No filename generation occurs.

             Input: echo * $PS2
                                echo "* $PS2"

`string`   Grave accents: The string is interpreted as a command.
             Instead of the original string, the result of the command
             is inserted in its place.

             Input: a=pwd
                                echo `$a`

\char   Backslash: The metacharacter following the blackslash
             loses its significance.

             Input: echo Good \<cr> Day
                                echo a\$"HOME\"

Examples:

        a=date
        echo $a   returns: "date"
        echo `$a`   returns the current date
        echo 'Date $a'   returns: "Date $a"
        echo "Date $a"   returns: "Date date"

Shell variables in procedures

There are special shell variables which are used only in procedures.
They also use a preceding dollar sign "$". The values in these variables
cannot be changed by simple assignment with the equal (=) character.
Of special practical significance are the position variables.

With the use of position variables, parameters can be passed to a shell
procedure. As in MS-DOS, the position variables are numbered zero
through nine, but MS-DOS uses a percent sign "%" instead of the dollar
sign "$".

The position variables have the following significance:

$0 =   Name of the calling shell procedure
$1 =   Parameter 1 (Argument) of the call
$2 =   Parameter 2 (Argument) of the call
$3 =   Parameter 3 (Argument) of the call
$4 =   Parameter 4 (Argument) of the call
$5 =   Parameter 5 (Argument) of the call
$6 =   Parameter 6 (Argument) of the call
$7 =   Parameter 7 (Argument) of the call
$8 =   Parameter 8 (Argument) of the call
$9 =   Parameter 9 (Argument) of the call

Note that position variables cannot be exported.

Example:

The following "mini" procedure will be called "xprint". It is used for sending the output of a file to the printer.

```
pr  -h  $2  $1  |  lp
```

The name of the file to be printed, and the headline, are passed to it as parameters (Arguments) during the call. Within the procedure, the name of the file can be found in Variable 1, which can be evaluated with $1. Variable 2 contains the desired headline.

Call the xprint procedure with:

```
sh  xprint  file1  "Headline"
```

Additional pre-defined variables, which contain information about processes, include:

$*   All arguments of the call in one character string
$@   All arguments of the call as individual character strings
$#   Number of positional arguments
$-   Options of the current shell
$?   Exit status of the last command executed
$$ Process number of the current shell
$!   Process number of the last background process

As an example, input:

```
echo $$
```

to examine the PID of the current shell.

The sample `xprint` shell, and for that matter any other shell procedure, can also be executed without the `sh` command. In this case, the user must have execution rights for the procedure file. The call can then be abbreviated as follows:

```
xprint  file1  "Headline"
```

Please note that `xprint` is a relative filename and must be available either in the working directory, or in a directory which is defined in the `PATH` shell variable.

Naming conventions of variables:

All shell variables which are not position variables, are called Keyword variable's.

Position variables can be assigned values with the `set` command, or by passing them through parameters (arguments) in the call (see the `xprint` example).

The `date` command returns date and time information, usually in the following form:

```
day_of_the_week, month, day, time, year
```

Test the effect of the `date` command on your system, it may differ in some small way.

Write the following `set_dat` procedure:

```
set  `date`
echo  $1  $2  $3  $4  $5  $6
echo  $*
echo  $#
echo  $$
```

Execute with:

```
sh set_dat   or:     set_dat     (x-right must exist!)
```

To establish execution access (x-right), the following one line `cx` procedure can be used:

```
chmod u+x $1
```

and executed with:

```
sh  cx  set_date
```

to set the user execution permission for the set_date procedure.

The general syntax of the set command is:

```
set [options] [parameter1 ....]
```

The set command, without options and parameters, outputs all the defined shell variables with their current values.

The set command options are referred to as shell options. The most important shell options are explained below:

-:   Setback of x and v.

e: Terminates the shell when the exit command status is not equal to 0.

k: Keyword variables can also follow the command name, or the name of the procedure (see below).

n: Syntax check only, no execution.

t: Execute the command in the current input line, then terminate the shell.

u: Unassigned variables are treated as errors.

v: All input lines are documented.

x: Commands and parameters are documented, except for, while, and until. Passing of variables can occur as follows:

> 1.   Export of shell variables
> 2.   In the procedure call:
>   a)   as a keyword variable
>   b)   as position variables

The passing of keyword variables

The following procedure is called test1 and the keyword variable is
"name". The procedure call would look like this:

```
name=Erna  sh  test1
```

The keyword variables, such as test1 in this example, must appear
before the procedure name, unless the -k option is set:

```
set  -k
sh  test1  name=Erna
```

The typical storage assignment of a subshell appears as follows:

Variable area:	1. Exported shell variables
	2. Keyword variables
	3. Variables defined in the process
Position variables	
Command portion	

All variables available automatically, can be displayed with the *env*
command.

With the command:

```
readonly  [variable1 ...]
```

Shell variables can be declared as constants that are valid until the
termination of the shell. Entering this command without any
arguments will output a listing of all readonly variables:

```
readonly
```

The shell variables can be erased by using the unset command with
UNIX System V:

```
unset VARNAME
```

Exercises:

1.)   Assign the shell variable HOME an existing directory.

      Make the home directory the working directory.

2.)   Assign the character string "input" to the first prompt character
      which is normally "$".

      a.   Start a subshell.

      b.   What has been determined?

3.)   Display all pre-defined shell variables.

12.3 Shell Programming

Shell procedures do not have to execute as a sequence of absolute commands. Shell procedures permit structures, such as if... then... else (selection) and while... do... done (loops).

Shell programming, with the help of such structures, can only be treated briefly in this introduction.

In general, the shell has all the characteristics of a higher level programming language, but not all problems can be solved on the shell level. Since the commands are interpreted (as in BASIC) rather than compiled, programs run relatively slow. Comprehensive application programs should be written in a compiler language such as C, Fortran or Cobol.

Shell programming offers a convenient method to perform repeated assignments effectively and with great flexibility. Characteristics of files, which are tested with special commands (such as test), often play an important role.

All UNIX commands can be used within a shell program. As a matter of fact, some commands such as test, sleep, eval and expr, are only sensible within shell procedures. Several of these commands test results for validity and return an exit status which can have the following values:

```
Exit-Status  = 0          (zero = true)
Exit-Status != 0          (not zero = false)
```

The most often used command of this type is test. For this reason, it will be discussed more extensively here.

TEST

Syntax: test expression   or,
                 [expression]   (not Berkeley)

The test command is used:

- to determine characteristics of files,
- compare character strings,
- compare whole numbers algebraically.

test returns the value "true" (exit status of 0) or "false" (exit status not equal to 0).

Expression:

-b name	name exists and is a block oriented device.
-c name	name exists and is a character oriented device.
-d name	name exists and is directory.
-f name	name exists and is a regular file.
-r name	name exists and is readable.
-s name	name exists and is not empty.
-n string	character string is not empty (length > 0).
-w name	name exists and is writable.
-x name	name exists and can be executed.
-z character	character string is empty (length = 0).
-z1 = z2	The two character strings, z1 and z2, are equal.
-z1 != z2	The two character strings, z1 and z2, are not equal.
val1 -op val2	The numeric values, val1 and val2, are compared on the basis of the operator. The operator (op) can be: eq, ne, gt, ge, lt, le (equal, not-equal, greater than, greater than or equal, less than, less than or equal).

Other expressions exist.

Conditions can be placed in parenthesis "(...)", negated with the exclamation mark "!", or connected logically with OR "-o" or AND "-a" operators.

Examples:

test -f name   True, if "name" exists and is a normal file.

test -d name   True, if "name" exists and is a directory.

test -f name -a -s name
                    True, if "name" exists as a normal file AND
                    "name" is not empty.

test -z "$a"   True, if the shell variable "a" contains an
                    empty character string (length equals zero).

test -n "$a"   True, if the shell variable "a" does not contain
                    an empty character string (non zero length).

test "$a" = "oma"
                    True, if the shell variable "a" contains the
                    character string "oma".

test "$a" -eq 1 -o "$a" -eq 2
                    True, if the shell variable "a" is 1 or 2.

test ! $# -eq 0   True, if the number of parameters of a shell
                    procedure is not equal to zero.

Caution: Avoid naming a file "test".

Exercise:

The following sequence occurs in a procedure:

```
abc=23
test "$abc" != 19
test "$abc" = 19
```

What is the exit status of the two test procedures?

The exit status can be determined with:

```
echo  $?
```

149

READ

Reads a complete line from `stdin` (file) and assigns the variables:

exit status = 0   read valid line
exit status = 1   EOF (End-of-File)

Example:

The command:

```
read a b c d
```

should read the following sentence as indicated:

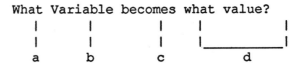

The criterion is the separator character. If more words exist than variables, the last variable gets the remaining words as a single character string. In this example, the last variable d is assigned the string "what value?"

EXPR

Can be used for arithmetic calculations with shell variables. Comparisons are also possible. During calculations, only whole numbers are permitted.

Syntax: `expr a op b`

The following logical operations (op) are permitted:

=	equal
<	smaller
>	greater
<=	smaller than or equal
>=	greater than or equal
! =	unequal

The following arithmetic operations (op) are permitted:

+	addition
–	subtraction
*	multiplication
/	division
%	mode (whole number remainder)

Verify the `expr` command through the following inputs:

```
a=6
b=5
c= `expr  $a = $b`
echo  $c              (c = 1 if the comparison was
                       successful, c = 0 if the comparison
                       was not successful)

expr  $a + 1
echo  $a
echo  `expr $a \< $b`
a= `expr  $a + 1`
b= `expr  $a  \*  $b`
echo  $a  $b
```

Note that the operators occurring in the examples, the less than "<" and asterisk "*", are also special characters of the shell. They must be neutralized with a backslash character "\" as shown in the example.

#, :, TRUE, FALSE, SLEEP

The commands #, :, true, false and sleep produce no output.

#	The rest of the command line is not read by the shell, allowing insertion of comments within the shell.
:	The empty command. This can be used to write comments into the procedure files with the help of arguments. (Caution: metacharacters of the shell are evaluated)!
true	Always returns the value "true" (exit status is zero).
false	Always returns the value "false" (exit status is not zero).
sleep n	Causes the shell to wait n seconds.

Write a procedure with the following content:

```
while true        # always true
do
  date
  sleep 5
done
```

This is the first shell procedure which uses a structure, in this case while... do... done. It outputs the date every five seconds on the screen. Since the condition always remains "true", the program executes an endless loop. How does the procedure have to be changed to make the waiting period variable?

The most important structures are:

IF... THEN... ELSE... FI

Syntax:

```
if condition              if condition
  then                      then
      commands                  commands
  else                      elif
      commands                then
  fi                            commands
                            else
                                commands
                          fi
```

Both of the formats shown are valid, and the "else" part in either format is optional.

Every command returns an exit status (or "return code"). The exit status is set by the current program and is:

- 0 for "true"
- not equal to 0 for "false"

The if construction can be nested further with elif as shown in the structure on the right above.

The following two examples determine if a file is a normal file or a directory. The filename must be the first argument.

Example 1:

```
1    if test -f $1
2    then
3      echo File $1 is a normal file
4    elif test -d $1
5      then
6        echo File $1 is a directory
7      else
8        echo File $1 does not exist
9    fi
```

Example 2:

```
 1    if test -z "$1"
 2    then
 3      echo Syntax error
 4    elif test -f $1
 5      then
 6        echo File $1 is a normal file
 7      elif test -d $1
 8        then
 9          echo File $1 is a directory
10        else
11          echo File $1 does not exist
12    fi
```

Exercise:

With the help of the `if... then... else` structure, write a procedure called "dat_1st" to output the contents of the file indicated in the call, the contents of the directory, or one of the following messages on the `stdout`:

```
File is a b-file
File is a c-file
File does not exist
```

The output of the file directory or the file can be sent to the printer if a variable "out" exists with the content "pr".

Note that under certain conditions the expression test may be missing. The indication of the option:

```
if test -f $1
```

can be written as:

```
if [ -f $1 ]
```

except on Berkeley systems.

Solution:

```
1     if [ -f $1 ]
2     then
3       if [ "$out" = pr ]
4       then
5         lp $1
6       else
7         more $1
8       fi
9     elif [ -d $1 ]
10    then
11      if [ "$out" = pr ]
12      then
13        ls -l $1 | lpr
14      else
15        ls -l $1
16      fi
17    else
18      if [ -b $1 ]
19      then
20        echo "File $1 is a b-device file"
21      else
22        if [ -c $1 ]
23        then
24          echo "File $1 is a c-device file"
25        else
26          echo "File $1 does not exist"
27        fi
28      fi
29    fi
```

Call: out=pr sh dat_lst filename   (to printer)

  sh dat_lst filename   (to display)

The previous procedure can also be done this way:

```
 1    if test -f $1
 2    then
 3      echo $1 " is a normal file" ; cat $1
 4      a=1
 5    else
 6      if test -d $1
 7      then
 8        echo $1 " is directory" ; ls -al $1
 9        a=2
10      else
11        if test -b $1
12        then
13          echo $1 " is b-device file"
14          a=3
15        else
16          if test -c $1
17          then
18            echo $1 " is c-device file"
19          a=4
20        else
21            echo " file does not exist"
22          fi
23        fi
24      fi
25    fi
26    if [ $2 = 1 ]
27    then
28      if [ $a = 1 ]
29      then
30        lp $1
31      fi
32      if [ $a = 2 ]
33      then
34        ls -al $1 | lp
35      fi
36    fi
```

Call: sh lst_dat filename 1   (to display and printer)
      sh lst_dat filename   (to display only)

Note that several commands can be written on a single line if they are
separated by a semicolon (as shown in lines 3 and 8 in the above
example).

WHILE... DO... DONE

Syntax:
```
while condition
do
   commands
done
```

The commands are executed until the exit status becomes "false".

Examples:

All arguments of a command line should be output:

```
while test -n "$1"
do
  echo $1
  shift
done
```

The `shift` command causes all arguments to be shifted left by one position. This makes it possible to address more than nine arguments.

The next example also determines if a file is a normal file or a directory. Again the filename is passed as the first argument:

```
1    while test -n "$1"
2    do
3      if test -f $1
4      then
5        echo File $1 is a normal file
6      elif test -d $1
7      then
8        echo File $1 is a directory
9      else
10       echo File $1 does not exist
11     fi
12     shift
13   done
```

Through the call of this shell procedure with "name" as the name of the procedure:

```
name *
```

A list of all files of the current directory is produced.

Exercises:

1.) Write a shell procedure with the call `work_1 a b`, which outputs the following:

```
                 Call:              work_1
Number of Arguments:              2
     Process number:              ...

         Argument #1:              a
         Argument #2:              b
                etc.
```

Keep the number of arguments and the procedure name flexible.

2.) Write a procedure which copies File1 into File2. The filename should be passed as a position parameter. The procedure should copy to several files by indicating several filenames.

Solutions:

```
to (1)   1   echo "Call: " $0
         2   echo "Number of Arguments: " $#
         3   echo "Process number: " $$
         4   echo
         5   a=1
         6   while [ "$1" != "" ]
         7   do
         8     echo $a". Argument: " $1
         9     shift
        10     a="`expr $a + 1`"
        11   done

     Call:   work_1 a b c d ...

to (2)   1   while test $2 != ''
         2   do cp $1 $2
         3     shift
         4   done

     Call:   work_2 dat1 dat2 dat3 dat4 ...
```

UNTIL... DO... DONE

Syntax: until condition
            do
                commands
            done

The until loop is the reverse of the while loop. The commands are executed until the exit status of the condition becomes "true".

Example:

The until loop can be used in command procedures to insure that the user takes the proper action. As an example, the following procedure runs until an existing filename is entered through the keyboard.

```
until test -f "$name"
do
  echo "Input:\c"
  read name
done
echo "File $name exists"
```

The first line can also be written as:

```
until [ -f "$name" ]
```

Exercise:

Write a shell procedure which calculates and outputs the quadratatic numbers (squares) from n to m. The values of n and m should be input parameters.

Solution:

```
1    a=$1
2    until [ "$a" -gt "$2" ]
3    do
4      erg="`expr $a \* $a`"
5      echo "The Square of $a is $erg"
6      a="`expr $a + 1`"
7    done
```

```
Call:       quad n m
```

Line 2 can also be written as:

```
until test $a -gt $e
```

FOR... IN... DO... DONE

Syntax: for word in string1 string2 ...
                   do
                       commands
                   done

The shell variable "word" is assigned successively string1, string2,... and the loop body is executed.

The for construction is not a counting loop as in many higher level programming languages.

Usually the return from a command is assigned to string1, string2,... for example `cat file`

Example:

```
for FILE in `find . -atime +90 -print`
do
   rm $FILE
done
```

The files of the current file directory for which no access occurred during the past 90 days are determined with the find command. These files are assigned consecutively to the shell variable "file" and then erased.

Exercise:

Write a procedure which searches a directory for empty files, writes the names into a control file, and erases the empty files in an interactive mode.

Solution:

```
1    cd $1
2    for word in `ls $1`
3    do
4      if [ ! -s $word -a -f $word ]
5      then
6        echo $word >>contr_leer
7        rm -i $word
8      fi
9    done
```

Call: proc [file directory]

Alternative solution:

```
1    ver=${1-.}
2    for file in `ls $ver`
3    do
4      if [ ! -s $file -a -f $file ]
5      then
6        echo $file >>contr_leer
7        rm -i $file
8      fi
9    done
```

In line 1, the content of the position variable "1" is assigned to the variable "ver". If it is empty, then "." is assigned as the content.

Some interesting and useful shell procedures can be found in Appendix C. A detailed explanation has been omitted, since some of the concepts exceed those presented so far.

13. Programming in C

The comments and examples about the C programming language that follow should not be misinterpreted as an introduction to the C language. This chapter is included only for demonstration purposes, to round out the overall view in this introduction to the UNIX environment.

C is closely tied to UNIX, which itself was written mostly in C. Therefore, C is normally referred to as the "native" language of UNIX. Many positive system characteristics can be used with programming in C. For example, the input and output redirection (Filter characteristics), and the pipe mechanism. Also, the basic UNIX command set can be enhanced through small C programs written by the user when desired. Several examples will be presented later for the extension of some of the standard UNIX commands.

C programs consist of function calls, at least one of which calls the function "main". The body of the function is enclosed in braces {...} as shown below:

Example 1: A simple example C program:

```
main()
{
    printf("My first C-Program \n");
}
```

To compile a C program, the UNIX command cc is used. Besides compiling the C source code, it also performs the linking operation to produce an executable program. Returning to the first example, the input to compile the program within the working directory would be:

```
cc prog1.c
```

The executable program generated by the compiler is automatically written to the file "a.out" in the same directory. The a.out program can be executed by entering a.out again. Of course, the a.out file would always be overwritten by the compilation of any C program in the same directory.

To prevent losing a previous output file, the executable program can be assigned a freely defined name through the use of the -o option of the cc command. The input:

```
cc -o prog1 prog1.c
```

would now cause the executable program to be stored in the `prog1` file. This program can be executed with the proper input.

In the second example that follows, the function "`text`" has been added. This function is called in the program (from the function "`main`") with its name, followed by parentheses. Within the parentheses, parameters can be indicated if the function is expecting data. This is not true for the "`text`" function. However, the parentheses, which are empty here, are still required even when no parameters are used.

Example 2:

```
main()
{
  text();
  text();
}
text()
{
  printf("Once is never \n");
}
```

Compilation and execution is similar to that used with the previous example 1.

C is a higher level language which has control structures, such as the `for` loop. A simple example of a `for` loop is presented in the next example. Note that the `for` loop in C is not related to the `for` construction of the shell!

Example 3:

```
main()
{
  int i;
  for(i=1; i<=10; i++)
    printf("%d  %d\n", i, i*i);
}
```

Variables must be declared in C programs. In this case only one variable, of the type `int` (Integer) exists. All variable declarations, and all executable commands, must be terminated by a semicolon. The `for` construction consists of three parts which are also separated by semicolons:

- Start value of the loop control variable,
- termination condition, and
- step increments of the loop control variable.

Note that the double plus sign "++" is a C specific operator, the increment operator, where:

```
i++;
```

is the equivalent of adding one to a variable and placing the result back in the same variable:

```
i=i+1;
```

`printf` is a function from the standard C library which is automatically linked to every program when needed. It's used to format output in a number of handy formats. Within the output string, each "`%d`" is a retainer (or conversion specification) for the space occupied by an integer variable. It indicates that the corresponding variable from the variable list (`i` or `i*i`) is to be output in decimal format. The "`\n`" indicates a line feed character is to be inserted at the end of each line.

The program in example 3 above calculates the square of the numbers from 1 to 10. The `printf` statement outputs each number and its square on a separate line.

As an added exercise, try using the `time` command to compare the execution time of the shell procedure (from the exercise used in the `Until... Do... Done` description) with the C program from example 3 above.

Almost all UNIX commands are written in C. The implementation of many of these commands is surprisingly short and simple, such as the `cp` (copy command):

Example 4:

```
#include <stdio.h>
main()
{
    int c;
    while ((c=getc(stdin)) != EOF)
        putc(c, stdout);
}
```

The `stdio.h` library, used in the `include` function above, contains a number of standard definitions and macros. Several of the more commonly used definitions are the End-of-File definition "EOF" and "!=" used as the "not equal" operator. Additionally, `stdio.h` includes `getc` and `putc`, which are standard functions to read or write an ASCII character to or from an indicated file (typically `stdin` and `stdout`).

Another characteristic of the C programming language will be demonstrated with a "do-it-yourself" `echo` command.

It is possible to pass arguments from the command line to the program being executed. For this purpose the `main` function must appear as follows:

```
main(argc, argv)
```

In the variable `argc` are the number of arguments from the command line, including the program name (command) itself.

The `argv` variable is a pointer to an array of character strings, with one command line argument per string. There is a "deeper" significance of this item, but it is not significant here. It's only important to know that there is a special variable type which must be declared with:

```
char *argv[];
```

The individual arguments passed to the program are then available in the `argv` array elements as character strings:

```
argv[1], argv[2], ..., argv[argc-1].
```

The name of the command itself can be found in `argv[0]`.

Note that the specific variable names argc and argv are not required, but are commonly used in most C programs.

The parameter passing mechanism closely resembles the position variables of the shell, as shown in the following example.

Example 5:

Enter this program, with a name of "xecho".

```
main(argc,argv)
int argc;
char *argv[];
{
  int i;
  for (i=1; i<argc; i++)  {
    printf("%s", argv[i] );
    printf(" ");
    }
  printf("\n");
}
```

Compile the program and try these examples:

```
echo   $HOME
xecho  $HOME
echo   "$HOME"
xecho  "$HOME"
echo   '$HOME'
xecho  '$HOME'
```

Also try entering:

```
a=date
echo   date
xecho  date
echo   `date`
xecho  `date`
```

The UNIX echo command and the C program xecho should behave identically.

Exercise, for experienced programmers:

There are a few four place numbers which produce the original number after they are split in the middle, and the two halves are squared and then added. They have the following form, where the letters A, B, C, and D can represent any four desired numbers, such as 3261:

```
ABCD    -->    (AB)*(AB) + (CD)*(CD)    =    ABCD
```

Write a program which finds these numbers and prints them out. Only a few of these numbers actually exist, and of course 3261 is not one of them! Note that the Division Operator is the slash "/", the Mode Operator is the percent sign "%" and the Equality Operator is the double equal sign "==" for the C programming language. It should be pointed out that the double equal sign is used to compare values, while the single equal sign is used to assign a value to a variable.

Also try writing the same program as a shell procedure. Then compare the execution times of the corresponding C program and shell procedure with the `time` command.

Solutions:

1.)   The numbers are: 1233   and: 8833

2.)   The following C program finds the four place numbers that fit the given equation.

```
main()
{
  int x, xl, xr;
  for (x=1000; x<10000; x++)    {
    xl = x / 100;
    xr = x % 100;
    if (xl*xl + xr*xr == x)
      printf(" n%d", x);
  }
}
```

14. What Else?

The basic information provided in this book should be a practical introduction to the use of the UNIX operating system on any computer system. Some theoretical aspects (general characteristics, file systems, process concept, etc.) were described more or less in greater detail when it was thought to be of help.

Most UNIX users will be able to work with the information acquired from this book. For others, it should not be difficult to obtain additional information from more detailed sources and advanced training courses. This should be true for any aspect of the system (such as additional commands, shell programming, the editors, etc.), including other special applications which must be handled under UNIX. Additionally, Appendix B contains a sorted list of many of the standard UNIX commands and utilities that can be found on most systems.

In closing, this final chapter will cover a few special tasks, including system administration, word processing and software development in the UNIX environment.

14.1 Tasks of the Super-users

Every UNIX system has a System Administrator who is usually called the super-user.

The System Administrator has the "root" user identification and the user number zero. In reality, the super-user is more of an institution than a person. Several persons can all be super-users. The super-user is the one who assigns and knows the proper passwords. He can bypass all safeguards, and even cause substantial damage. For this reason, the password of the System Administrator should not be generally known. If the super-user has forgotten his own password, the UNIX system must be installed again as soon as system administration tasks are required. The System Administrator is responsible for the reliable operation of the overall system.

Among the System Administrator's tasks are:

- Administration of the super-user password

- Implementation of new user identifications

- Display of daily messages (motd)

- Implementation of new User Groups

- Control of disk assignments

- Data security

- Emergency interventions

- Configuration of the system

- Installation of new software products

If the user has forgotten his password, or has other problems with the system, the super-user should be contacted.

On most systems, the super-user will have a collection of special commands at his disposal which can be used with shell procedures to make his assignment tasks easier.

14.2 Word Processing with UNIX

Word processing is important under UNIX, but has lost some significance since the appearance of modern PC word processing programs such as MS-WORD, WordPerfect, and others. The capabilities offered by UNIX in this area are still unsurpassed, but unfortunately they're still complicated to use. It should be kept in mind that the UNIX tools, compared with the PC products, are fairly old.

UNIX offers many word processing and text formatting tools, but in general they can only be used through complicated pipelines and procedures. They are not for the occasional letter writer or clerk-typist. From the many available text tools, some of the most important include:

`nroff`	Formatting program for display and printer output
`troff`	Formatting program for phototypesetting output
`ms`	For the development of technical or scientific documents
`eqn`	Program to produce mathematical formulas
`pic`	Used for the creation of simple graphics
`tbl`	Table generating program

Several other generally useful tools such as `comm`, `grep` and `sort` have been discussed already.

14.3   Program Development with UNIX

UNIX was initially a special operating system for software developers. This characteristic is still an advantage for UNIX today.

The developer has about 60 system calls available which help to develop "turnkey" systems. Together with many other characteristics, such as the start procedure, filter and pipelines, and controlled file access; the user has a tailored application area. The user does not have to leave his application since even the interrupt key can be intercepted and redirected.

To return to the software developer. He has a series of compilers available under UNIX, such as C, Pascal, Fortran and Cobol. This in itself is nothing special since other operating systems also offer them. The one important factor is the close connection between UNIX and the higher level language C, as shown in chapter 13. The C language permits "bit fiddling" which generally can only be performed with an Assembler. C is also a structured programming language, with efficient set and file management in contrast with Assemblers. Those who have chosen the UNIX environment should not ignore C!

Besides the shell procedures, the filters, pipelines and compilers, UNIX offers a series of special tools for software development.

Source Code Control System (SCCS):

Special mention should be made of the Source Code Control System (SCCS). It is used for the control of text files which are closely connected with program development, mainly for source code files and program documentation. The use of SCCS is highly recommended for the development of very large software systems, especially when several individuals are working jointly on a project. SCCS makes it easier to administer text files, and to find or rebuild older versions of any file. The files are first stored with their original contents. Then, only the changes relative to the previous version are stored with each revision. This method saves space while documenting every level of change.

The order and security gained through the use of SCCS comes at a high price in administration and time expenditure. If a certain version is to be reconstructed, all preceding versions must be processed.

Makefile:

Another tool can be used to maintain logically connected file groups. They can be modules of a large software system, or any other group of interdependent files within the system. A control file called the "Makefile" records what files are dependent on, or built from, other files within the system. Whenever any of the dependent files are changed, the Make command is executed and all affected files are re-processed as indicated in the appropriate Makefile.

The use of the Makefile can save significant time by only processing the files that need to be recompiled, relinked, etc. The Makefile also insures that the final product is always correct and up to date, with the proper versions included for every file used to construct the total package.

As a simple example:

The program prog1 consists of modules mod1 and mod2, with the corresponding source files mod1.c and mod2.c. If mod2.c is changed, this requires two courses of action to follow:

1.)   mod2.c must be compiled

2.)   prog1 must be linked

These steps are performed automatically by executing make with the corresponding Makefile.

As you would guess, a simple problem such as this would not require the use of the Makefile capabilities. Similar to SCCS, it is generally used only in connection with large or complicated systems.

Appendix A   ASCII-Table

Dec	Hex	Oct	Binary	ASCII	Meaning
0	00	0	00000000	^@ NUL	Null
1	01	1	00000001	^A SOH	Start Of Heading
2	02	2	00000010	^B STX	Start Of Text
3	03	3	00000011	^C ETX	End Of Text
4	04	4	00000100	^D EOT	End Of Transmission
5	05	5	00000101	^E ENQ	Inquiry
6	06	6	00000110	^F ACK	Acknowledge
7	07	7	00000111	^G BEL	Bell
8	08	10	00001000	^H BS	Backspace
9	09	11	00001001	^I HT	Horizontal Tab
10	0A	12	00001010	^J LF	Line Feed
11	0B	13	00001011	^K VT	Vertical Tab
12	0C	14	00001100	^L FF	Form Feed
13	0D	15	00001101	^M CR	Carriage Return
14	0E	16	00001110	^N SO	Shift Out
15	0F	17	00001111	^O SI	Shift In
16	10	20	00010000	^P DLE	Data Link Escape
17	11	21	00010001	^Q DC1	Device Contr.1 (X-ON)
18	12	22	00010010	^R DC2	Device Contr.2 (TAPE)
19	13	23	00010011	^S DC3	Device Contr.3 (X-OFF)
20	14	24	00010100	^T DC4	Device Contr.4 (TAPE)
21	15	25	00010101	^U NAK	Negative Acknowledge
22	16	26	00010110	^V SYN	Synchronous Idle
23	17	27	00010111	^W ETB	End Of Transmission Block
24	18	30	00011000	^X CAN	Cancel
25	19	31	00011001	^Y EM	End Of Medium
26	1A	32	00011010	^Z SUB	Substitute
27	1B	33	00011011	ESC	Escape
28	1C	34	00011100	^\ FS	File Separator
29	1D	35	00011101	^] GS	Group Separator
30	1E	36	00011110	^~ RS	Record Separator
31	1F	37	00011111	^/ US	Unit Separator
32	20	40	00100000	SP	Space
33	21	41	00100001	!	Exclamation Point
34	22	42	00100010	"	Quotation Mark
35	23	43	00100011	#	Number Sign
36	24	44	00100100	$	Dollar Sign
37	25	45	00100101	%	Percent Sign
38	26	46	00100110	&	Ampersand
39	27	47	00100111	'	Apostrophe

Dec	Hex	Oct	Binary	ASCII	Meaning
40	28	50	00101000	(	Opening Parenthesis
41	29	51	00101001	)	Closing Parentheses
42	2A	52	00101010	*	Asterisk
43	2B	53	00101011	+	Plus
44	2C	54	00101100	,	Comma
45	2D	55	00101101	–	Hyphen (Minus)
46	2E	56	00101110	.	Period (Decimal)
47	2F	57	00101111	/	Slash (Division)
48	30	60	00110000	0	
49	31	61	00110001	1	
50	32	62	00110010	2	
51	33	63	00110011	3	
52	34	64	00110100	4	
53	35	65	00110101	5	
54	36	66	00110110	6	
55	37	67	00110111	7	
56	38	70	00111000	8	
57	39	71	00111001	9	
58	3A	72	00111010	:	Colon
59	3B	73	00111011	;	Semicolon
60	3C	74	00111100	<	Less Than
61	3D	75	00111101	=	Equal
62	3E	76	00111110	>	Greater Than
63	3F	77	00111111	?	Question Mark
64	40	100	01000000	@	Commercial At Sign
65	41	101	01000001	A	
66	42	102	01000010	B	
67	43	103	01000011	C	
68	44	104	01000100	D	
69	45	105	01000101	E	
70	46	106	01000110	F	
71	47	107	01000111	G	
72	48	110	01001000	H	
73	49	111	01001001	I	
74	4A	112	01001010	J	
75	4B	113	01001011	K	
76	4C	114	01001100	L	
77	4D	115	01001101	M	
78	4E	116	01001110	N	
79	4F	117	01001111	O	
80	50	120	01010000	P	
81	51	121	01010001	Q	

Dec	Hex	Oct	Binary	ASCII	Meaning
82	52	122	01010010	R	
83	53	123	01010011	S	
84	54	124	01010100	T	
85	55	125	01010101	U	
86	56	126	01010110	V	
87	57	127	01010111	W	
88	58	130	01011000	X	
89	59	131	01011001	Y	
90	5A	132	01011010	Z	
91	5B	133	01011011	[	Opening Bracket
92	5C	134	01011100	\	Backslash
93	5D	135	01011101	]	Closing Bracket
94	5E	136	01011110	^	Circumflex
95	5F	137	01011111	_	Underscore
96	60	140	01100000	`	Grave Accent
97	61	141	01100001	a	
98	62	142	01100010	b	
99	63	143	01100011	c	
100	64	144	01100100	d	
101	65	145	01100101	e	
102	66	146	01100110	f	
103	67	147	01100111	g	
104	68	150	01101000	h	
105	69	151	01101001	i	
106	6A	152	01101010	j	
107	6B	153	01101011	k	
108	6C	154	01101100	l	
109	6D	155	01101101	m	
110	6E	156	01101110	n	
111	6F	157	01101111	o	
112	70	160	01110000	p	
113	71	161	01110001	q	
114	72	162	01110010	r	
115	73	163	01110011	s	
116	74	164	01110100	t	
117	75	165	01110101	u	
118	76	166	01110110	v	
119	77	167	01110111	w	
120	78	170	01111000	x	
121	79	171	01111001	y	
122	7A	172	01111010	z	
123	7B	173	01111011	{	Opening Brace

Dec	Hex	Oct	Binary	ASCII	Meaning
124	7C	174	01111100	|	Verticle Line (Pipe)
125	7D	175	01111101	}	Closing Brace
126	7E	176	01111110	~	Tilde
127	7F	177	01111111	DEL	Delete (Rubout)

Appendix B   Standard UNIX Utilities

The following list provides a sorted index of many of the more common UNIX utilities and commands available on most systems:

`accept`	Permits spooling requests for printer
`adb`	Absolute debugger
`ar`	Maintains portable archives and libraries
`as`	Assembler
`at`	Executes commands at a later time
`awk`	Pattern scanning and processing language
`banner`	Makes text banners
`basename`	Outputs file name from path name
`batch`	Executes commands at a later time
`bc`	Desktop calculator with programming constructs and arbitrary precision
`bdiff`	Compares two large files
`bfs`	Big file scanner
`cal`	Outputs calendar
`calendar`	Appointment scheduler
`cancel`	Cancels previous spool request
`cat`	Concatenates and prints files
`cc`	C language compiler
`cd`	Changes current working directory
`chgrp`	Changes group ownership of file or directory
`chmod`	Changes file access permissions
`chown`	Changes file ownership
`cmp`	Compares two files
`col`	Filters reverse line feeds
`comm`	Selects or rejects lines common to two sorted files
`cp`	Copies files
`cpio`	Copies files archives in and out
`cpp`	C language preprocessor
`crypt`	Encodes and decodes files
`csplit`	Splits files based on pattern matching
`ct`	Spawns a getty process to a remote terminal
`ctrace`	Traces C program execution
`cu`	Calls another UNIX system
`cut`	Cuts out selected fields of each line of a file
`cxref`	Generates C program cross-reference listing
`date`	Sets or prints the current date
`dc`	Desktop calculator
`dd`	Performs file transformations

`deroff`	Removes formatting commands from file
`df`	Displays free space in file system
`diff`	Compares two files
`diff3`	Compares three files
`dircmp`	Compares directories
`dirname`	Outputs the path from a path name
`dis`	Object file disassembler
`disable`	Disables spooling on printer
`du`	Summarizes disk usage
`echo`	Echoes arguments
`ed, edit`	Line-oriented editors
`enable`	Enables spooling on a printer
`env`	Sets environment for command execution
`expr`	Evaluates arguments as an expression
`factor`	Obtains prime factors of a number
`fgrep`	Searchs a file for a character string
`file`	Determines file type
`find`	Searches for files
`fsdb`	Debugs damaged file systems
`ged`	Graphical editor
`getopts`	Parses command line options
`glossary`	Displays definitions of UNIX system terms and symbols
`graph`	Draws a graph
`graphics`	Accesses graphical and numerical commands
`greek`	Selects terminal filter
`grep`	Selects lines of a file based on pattern matching
`gutil`	Graphical utilities
`help`	Provides on-line help on UNIX commands
`helpadm`	Makes changes to the Help Facility database
`id`	Outputs user and group ID's and names
`ipcs`	Reports interprocess communication facilities status
`join`	Joins two tabular data files
`kill`	Terminates or signals a process
`line`	Copies a line from standard input to output
`ln`	Links file names
`login`	Admits authorized users to system
`logname`	Outputs the user's login name
`lp, lpr`	Line printer spooler
`lpadmin`	Configures the `lp` spooling system
`lpstat`	Printer spooling status information
`ls`	Lists contents of directories

m4	Macro processor
mail	Sends and receives UNIX mail
mailx	Extended mail facility
make	Regenerates groups of programs
makekey	Generates encryption key
man	Prints on-line manual entries
mesg	Permits or denies messages
mkdir	Makes a directory
mkfs	Creates a file system on disk
mknod	Creates a directory entry for a special file
mount	Mounts a file system
mv	Moves files
mvdir	Moves a directory
newform	Reformats lines of a text file
newgrp	Changes active group membership
news	Prints news items
nice	Runs a program at reduced priority
nl	Line numbering filter
nohup	Runs a command immune from hang-ups and quits
nroff	Text formatter
od	Outputs an octal dump of a file
pack	Packs files
passwd	Changes a user's login password
paste	Merges lines of files
pcat	Concatenates packed files
pg	Browse file contents on terminal screen
pr	Prints files
ps	Outputs process status
pwd	Prints the name of the current working directory
rm	Removes files
rmdir	Removes directories
rsh	Restricted UNIX system shell
sag	Outputs system activity graph
sar	Outputs system activity report
scat	Concatenates and prints files
sdb	Symbolic debugger
sdiff	Compares two files
sed	Stream editor
sh	The UNIX system shell
shl	Shell layer manager
shutdown	Shuts down the system
sleep	Suspends execution for a time interval
sort	Sorts and merges files

split	Splits a file
starter	Displays UNIX information for new users
strip	Removes symbol table information from an object file
stty	Sets terminal characteristics
su	Temporarily changes user-ID
sum	Outputs checksum and block count for a file
sync	Writes disk buffers to disk
sysadm	Menu driven system administration utility
tabs	Sets tabs on a terminal
tail	Outputs the last part of a file
tar	Tape file archiver
tee	Pipe fitter
test	Evaluates conditions
time	Times command execution
touch	Updates access and modification times of a file
tr	Character translation filter
troff	Phototypesetter text formatter
true	Returns true value
tty	Outputs name of a terminal
umask	Sets file creation mode mask
umount	Dismounts a file system
uname	Outputs the name of the current UNIX system
uniq	Outputs a file with unique lines
units	Performs units conversions
unpack	Unpacks packed files
usage	Displays information about command usage
uucp	Copies files between UNIX systems
uulog	Outputs uucp log information
uuname	Outputs uucp names of known systems
uustat	Outputs uucp status information
uux	Executes a command on a remote UNIX system
vi	Full screen text editor
wait	Waits for completion of background processes
wall	Sends a message to all users
wc	Outputs line, word and character counts for a file
who	Outputs information on current users
write	Sends messages to another user
xargs	Constructs an argument list and executes a command
yacc	Compiler-generating tool

Appendix C   Useful Shell Procedures

Several shell procedures are listed in this Appendix which can be executed on your system. You may find one or more of them to be useful.

Some of the constructions used will exceed the material covered in this book. For example, in the bigclk procedure the following command is used:

```
PAUSE="{$1-60}"
```

The positional variable $1 is normally assigned a passed parameter. If it is missing, "60" is assigned as the default value.

For the following shell procedures, only the overall function of the procedure will be explained. The significance of individual commands used within the procedure will not be discussed.

Shell Procedure: bigclk

Creates a digital clock on the screen (stdout) which is updated at the specified interval in seconds.

```
        #
#  bigclk - creates digital clock
#
IFS=" :"
PAUSE="{$1-60}"
DPAUSE="`expr $PAUSE + 2 `"
while true
do
   clear
   set `date`
   DATUM="`banner $4-$5-$6 `"
   cat <<EOF
*********************************************************
*********************************************************
*********************************************************
   $DATUM
*********************************************************
*********************************************************
*********************************************************
END with DEL - Display changes: Every $DPAUSE  seconds
   EOF
   sleep $PAUSE
done
```

Call: bigclk   sec

Example: bigclk 10   Clock is updated every 10 seconds

              bigclk   Clock is updated every 60 seconds

Note that the banner command may not be available on all systems. Usually it can be found in the /usr/bin directory.

Sample output of `bigclk`:

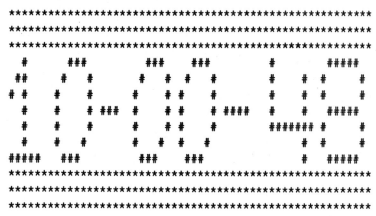

```
************************************************************
************************************************************
************************************************************
    #       ###         ###     ###           #         #####
   ##      #   #       #   #   #   #           #       #   #     #
  # #     #   #       #   # #     #           #       #   #     #
    #     #   # ###   #     # #     # ####   #       #   #####
    #     #   #       #     # #     #       #######  #         #
    #     #   #       #   # #     #           #   #     #
  #####   ###         ###     ###           #     #####
************************************************************
************************************************************
************************************************************
```
END with DEL - Display changes: Every 60 seconds

Shell Procedure: list

This procedure uses only known commands. It creates a list with four digit line numbers for the printout of files such as source programs. The list procedure reads from stdin and writes to stdout (filter).

Example of an application:

```
list <cprog.c | lp
```

In this procedure, IFS=@ sets the field separator to a dummy value so that a complete line is assigned to the variable line.

```
#
#   list - adds line numbers to output files
#
IFS=@
a=0
while read line
do
    a=`expr $a + 1`
    if [ $a -lt 10 ]
    then
        echo "000$a $line"
    else
        if [ $a -lt 100 ]
        then
            echo "00$a $line"
        else
            if [ $a -lt 1000 ]
            then
                echo "0$a $line"
            else
                if [ $a -ge 1000 ]
                then
                    echo "$a $line"
                fi
            fi
        fi
    fi
done
```

Shell Procedure: tree

Call: `tree [directory]`

The function of this procedure is similar to the `tree` command of MS-DOS. The file `tree`, starting at the directory indicated, is output (on `stdout`). If no directory is indicated, the starting point is the working directory.

Directories are marked with preceding and following dashes "--.....--" to differentiate them from normal files.

```
#
# tree - generates a directory structure
# recursively
#
CALL="Call: $0 [directory] [platz]"
DIR=${1-`pwd`}; export DIR
echo "$2--$DIR--"
PLACE="$2      "
cd $DIR
for i in `ls`
do
    if [ -d "$i" ]
    then
        echo $0 "$i" "$PLACE"
    else
        echo "$PLACE$i"
    fi
done
exit 0
```

Sample output of `tree`:

```
--/u2/pae--
  --Q0--
    default.f
    dict.dat
    --lej--
    pit1base.dat
    pitmask.f
    --tmp--
      test1
      understand
    --unix--
      dbinfo
      preise.txt
    unix.np
  --bases--
    --peter.dbs--
      adr___100.dat
      adr___100.idx
```

Shell Procedure: cpdir

Call: cpdir fromdir todir

Copies a complete file branch to another location in the file tree. The
"todir" directory must exist (use mkdir if required).

```
#
#  cpdir - copies complete file branches
#
if test "$#" -ne "2"
then
    echo Call $0: $0 fromdir todir
    exit 1
elif test ! -d "$1"
then
    echo $0: $1 is not a directory
    exit 1
elif test ! -d "$2"
then
    echo $0: $2 is not a directory
    exit 1
fi
TODIR="$2"
echo "$0 from $1 to $2 ...\\c"
cd $1
find . -depth -print | cpio -pdl $2
echo "done"
echo "Compare files \\c"
set `find . -type f -print | sed "s\..\\\" `
for file
do
    if cmp $file $TODIR/$file
    then
        # do nothing
    else
        echo error in verification of the file $file
        echo please check
        exit 1
    fi
done
echo ".....ok"
exit 0
```

191

Shell Procedure:　lockterm

Locks the display to prevent use by others until the input of a password
(which is input without echoing characters).

```
#
#       lockterm - locks the display
#
trap "stty echo" 0
trap "" 1 2 3 15
echo "Password:\c"
stty -echo
read PASSWD DUMMY
if [ -z "$PASSWD" ]
then
    exit 1
fi
clear
echo Screen is locked !!!
echo ""
echo ""
echo "Password please:\c"
read OPASSWD DUMMY
while [ "$PASSWD" != "$OPASSWD" ]
do
    clear
    echo Screen is locked !!!
    echo ""
    echo ""
    echo "Password please:\c"
    read OPASSWD DUMMY
done
clear
exit 0
```

Shell Procedure:　loginsh

Call: `sh loginsh`

Searches for the process number of the user's login shell.

In this simple manner, the PID of the user's own login shell can be determined and can then be terminated with the `kill` command. This terminates all following child processes.

```
#
#       loginsh
#
trap "" 1 2 3 15
FILE=/tmp/ps$$
trap "rm $FILE" 0
ps -lu $LOGNAME >$FILE
exec <$FILE
while read LINE
do
    set $LINE
    if [ "$5" -eq "1" ]
    then
        echo $4
        exit 0
    fi
done
echo 0
exit 1
```

Index

Abacus pc catalog

Order Toll Free 1-800-451-4319

5370 52nd Street SE • Grand Rapids, MI 49512
Phone: (616) 698-0330 • Fax: (616) 698-0325

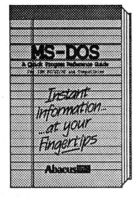